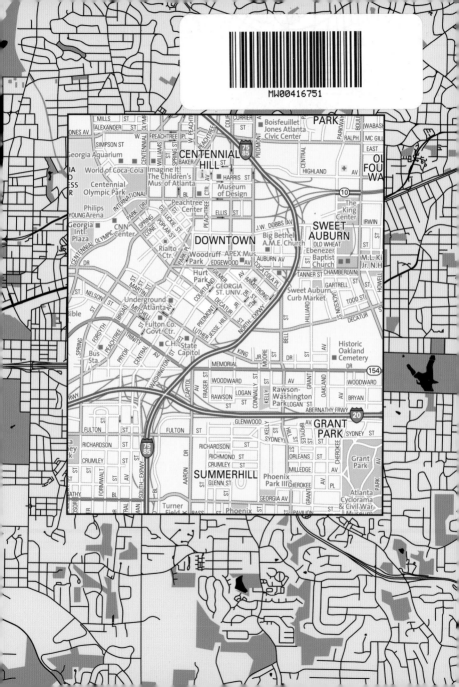

ATLANTA
COCKTAILS

AN ELEGANT COLLECTION
OF OVER 100 RECIPES
INSPIRED BY GEORGIA'S CAPITAL

TRISHA PINTAVORN

CIDER MILL PRESS

BOOK PUBLISHERS

ATLANTA COCKTAILS

ISBN-13: 978-1-40034-485-7
ISBN-10: 1-4003-4485-9

This book may be ordered by mail from the publisher. Please include $5.99 for postage and handling. Please support your local bookseller first!

Books published by Cider Mill Press Book Publishers are available at special discounts for bulk purchases in the United States by corporations, institutions, and other organizations. For more information, please contact the publisher.

Cider Mill Press Book Publishers
"Where good books are ready for press"
501 Nelson Place
Nashville, Tennessee 37214
cidermillpress.com

Typography: Haboro Contrast, Copperplate, Sackers, Warnock

Photography credits on page 374

Printed in India

24 25 26 27 28 REP 5 4 3 2 1

First Edition

CONTENTS

INTRODUCTION

Welcome to Atlanta, Where the Players Play

Atlanta is a big deal today, but in the year of its birth, 1837, it was a different story. Atlanta was simply a random spot on the map picked out to be nothing more than a humble railroad junction, good "for one tavern, a blacksmith shop, a grocery store, and nothing else." Jump to today, it's now a powerhouse by nearly every conceivable measure.

You can see in the city's ever-expanding skyline that it's an economic shining star, the headquarters to a roster of global brands like Delta Airlines, UPS, and Coca-Cola. World-renowned colleges and universities like Morehouse, Emory, and Georgia Tech have made this city their home. The birthplace of Martin Luther King Jr., Atlanta was the heartbeat of the Civil Rights Movement in the 1960s. Today, it is an incredibly diverse and beautiful mosaic of native Atlantans and transplants from all over Georgia, the Southeast, and beyond.

In Atlanta, we love our sports teams through good times and bad. The Braves have won the World Series four times now, and the Atlanta Hawks and Atlanta United have had some amazing wins, too. And as Falcons fans, we've also been through some things together . . . unspeakable things . . . but we'll never stop cheering on the Dirty Birds.

Atlanta is also known for being a cultural epicenter. It's a veritable hotbed for some of the most talented Grammy award-winning rap and R&B artists in history. A petition to replace the Stone Mountain Confederate Memorial with a monument to rap duo Outkast (we'll never stop being obsessed with them) gained thousands of signatories. Thanks to a generous tax provision, countless films and TV shows have been filmed here, from Netflix's *Stranger Things* to Donald Glover's *Atlanta*. You'll also see from time to time people throughout the city wearing sweatshirts and ball caps with the phrase, "Atlanta Influences Everything" stitched across the front. And we believe it!

So when it comes to the city's drinking scene? It's even hotter than a July afternoon in Atlanta.

A Brief History of Cocktails in Atlanta

Atlanta's attitudes toward drinking, however, have ebbed and flowed with history. As was brilliantly chronicled by authors Mary Boyle and Ron Smith in *Prohibition in Atlanta: Temperance, Tiger Kings & White Lightning* (2015), rum punch was the original drink of choice for colonial Georgia, and by the early 1800s, Atlanta had become a rather raucous place. A wild frontier town, Atlanta and its riotous Decatur Street in particular were filled with gambling, drunken brawls, and prostitution, with the drinks of choice being brandy, Madeira wine, and crudely made corn whiskey.

Decatur Street, 1864

"Marching Through Georgia," 1908 Prohibition art, L.M. Glackens

Atlanta had its first official flirtation with the Prohibition movement when a short-lived ban on liquor sales took effect in 1885. Like a lot of Prohibition laws in the country, this ban had all sorts of loopholes which made it laughably unsuccessful. It didn't go into effect immediately, so people simply stocked up on jugs or even barrels of whiskey. Domestically made wines were still allowed, and it was easy enough, with a wink and a nod, to have a nonalcoholic beverage swapped out for the real stuff in the backrooms of certain establishments. This law was repealed just two years later, but not before a clever Atlanta pharmacist invented a little drink you may have heard of called Coca-Cola. This cocaine-infused concoction was marketed as a "temperance drink," and it is now consumed 1.8 billion times daily—sans the cocaine, that is.

Eventually, the entire state of Georgia would undergo an alcohol ban from 1907 to 1935—a whopping twenty-five years. One likely impetus for this statewide ban was the 1906 Atlanta race riots during which a mob of upwards of 10,000 white Americans went on a violent rampage. The mob killed many innocents and destroyed the racially integrated Decatur Street saloons often frequented by African Americans, which prohibitionists blamed as being hotbeds for crime. With the 1907 ban, dozens more saloons shuttered their doors, and Atlanta-based spirits distillers like R.M. Rose had to pack up and move out of the state. R.M. Rose had sold not only liquors, but a number of bottled cocktails at the time, like a Martini and a concoction called the Wild Cherry Cordial and Rum ("fine in case of colds or grippe") for a dollar each. But some years after relocating to Chattanooga, R.M. Rose went bankrupt, and it'd be another 100 years before Atlanta had its next liquor distillery.

Asa Candler, Coca-Cola
king of Atlanta, 1923

In the 1920s, Atlanta didn't necessarily have the sexy, rowdy speakeasy culture that places like New York City experienced. However, drinking was absolutely present. A survey done by *Collier's* magazine in 1925 proclaimed Atlanta to be the wettest city in the nation. In Atlanta during this time, drinking seemed to be relegated to a hip flask, with a bit of alcohol nipped by young people in the privacy of their homes, during football games, or at dances.

Fast-forward to the 1960s, and Atlanta's nightlife scene was beginning to reach a fever pitch. Atlanta's longest-running strip club, the Clermont Lounge, found its footing during this time and is still beloved today.

In the 1970s, the drinking age was lowered to 18, leading to a raucous decade where bright, disco-colored drinks were all the rage. The legendary Limelight nightclub in Atlanta opened—the "Studio 54 of the South"—where celebrities like Tina Turner, Grace Jones, and Andy Warhol famously partied. The ingredients definitely weren't high-quality, but boy, did folks have a good time funneling back Singapore Slings and Hurricanes at the Underground Atlanta. Cream-based drinks like Brandy Alexanders and White Russians were also popular. Tiki culture found its way to Atlanta as well in this decade with Trader Vic's, which is still slinging Mai Tais today.

Gay nightclubs and drag bars flourished, and Tequila Sunrises had a moment in the 1980s. Lemon Drops and other drinks made possible by those god-awful pre-packaged sour mixes ruled the 2000s bar and club scene, while Hunch Punch, a potent mix of Everclear and Hawaiian Punch, was a staple at Atlanta's colleges.

All this is to say that, despite a hard-partying past, it truly wasn't until the past two decades that Atlanta's modern craft cocktail scene began to emerge. But we sure have made up for lost time.

Trends in Atlanta Cocktail Culture Today

For the past decade and a half, there's been a real rise and dedication to craft cocktails, trailblazed by industry titans like Ticonderoga Club's Greg Best and Paul Calvert and Kimball House's Miles Macquarrie. Today, the Atlanta cocktail scene is simply better than it ever has been.

"Twenty years ago, I'd travel and I was blown away every time; fifteen years ago, a little less; ten years ago, a little less, and now Atlanta is one of the best cities in the country for cocktails," says Michael Gallagher of LEON's Full Service. SOS Tiki Bar's Ian Jones agrees: "I think a lot of people think Atlanta is a secondary-tier city, but when I go to other cities, I go, 'We have the same thing in Atlanta, and it doesn't cost me $30.'"

Part of that is a greater emphasis on natural, good-for-you ingredients in cocktails that bartenders are really embracing in Atlanta. The "crazy color schemes [in cocktails] of the 1970s, those wild greens, yellows, purples, blues that are just totally unnatural, we're finding ways to do this naturally," using ingredients like spirulina and "hibiscus flowers to make beautiful reds and pinks," says Ian Mendelsohn, the beverage director at Fifth Group Atlanta.

Brunch in Atlanta is now huge, too. And with it, at last, booze! Up until 2018, you famously could not order a drink on Sundays before 12:30 p.m. in Georgia, but the "Brunch Bill" now lets you enjoy a passion fruit Mimosa alongside your chicken and waffles beginning at 11 a.m. on Sundays.

Presentation, of course, is key. This is where you can really see Atlanta's stylish swagger beginning to appear in the cocktail scene. "Your cocktail needs to be photo-ready, just like your outfit," says The James

Room's Harold Brinkley. Liquid nitrogen bubbles, gold flakes, and smoked Old Fashioneds abound in Atlanta. We're a city known for being full of stunters and hustlers, so it's no surprise we like a little glitz and glam in our drinks, too.

But the drinking scene in Atlanta is also incredibly unserious and playful. On a sunny Saturday afternoon on Atlanta's BeltLine, you're going to find tons of people sipping on the adult version of a Capri Sun on the patio of the bar Ladybird. A whiskey-and-Coke frozen slushie has long been the go-to drink at Victory Sandwich Bar. We also can't resist a cheekily named drink—head to Twisted Soul Kitchen & Bar for a "Southernplayalisticadillacmuzik" or to Aye Tea Elle for a "Black Girl Magic." We have an insane amount of Christmas pop-up bars, too, where the whole draw seems to be that you can enjoy torched marshmallows as your garnish and drink your eggnog out of a Santa-shaped cup. It may be silly, but we love it!

Where you'll find great cocktails in Atlanta, you'll also likely find great food, too. Complex liquor laws make it easier for many places in Atlanta to operate as a brewpub, which means that 50% of profits must be from the sales of food. So, don't overlook this city's restaurants if you're in search of a great drink!

Another mistake you don't want to make is pigeonholing Atlanta as simply a Southern city. This metropolis is a hub for global flavors and influences. So yes, you'll find cocktails made with local produce and ingredients, from moonshine flavored with peach to craft cocktails made with peanut orgeat. But you will also find globally inspired offerings, from agave spirits to the finest Japanese whiskeys, oftentimes brought here by the first- and second-generation immigrant populations from all over the world who now call ATL home.

Lastly, you don't want to miss out on gems in Atlanta's suburbs. There's just no getting around the metropolitan sprawl that is Atlanta. The number of people who live in the official city of Atlanta is less than 500,000, yet nearly six million people call the metro area home. Gentrification has also pushed tons of talented small business owners out into the 'burbs, so it's silly to limit yourself to only your area. Atlanta's I-285 highway, which encircles the official city limits, often serves as the dividing line, with neighborhoods outside of the perimeter called "OTP" and neighborhoods inside called "ITP." I am firmly in the camp that a great gem is a great gem, whether it's in Decatur or College Park or Duluth, and you'll see the best of the best from all over the metro area represented in this book.

When it comes to original creations, it is true that we don't yet have an iconic invention like New York's Manhattan or New Orleans's Sazerac. But bartenders around ATL have a few ideas for what you could say is Atlanta's signature drink. A beer and a shot will always be popular. The Old Fashioned has long been king, and you'll find plenty of excellent riffs in this book. But agave spirits are fast on the rise, too. "Maybe a Margarita with a lemon pepper rim" is something that Katie McDonald, beverage director and partner of Banshee in East Atlanta, jokingly guesses could become our signature cocktail. (I was delighted to find through the course of this book that at least two interpretations of Atlanta's favorite food—the lemon pepper wing—do indeed exist, at Lazy Betty and Gunshow.)

However, the fact that there's no clear consensus shows that Atlanta's drink scene is still growing, flowing, and evolving. There's no shortage of talented mixologists hungry to make their mark on The A. So, without further ado, let's dive into this wonderful city that I call home.

How to Stock Your Home Bar Like You're from Atlanta

A well-stocked bar, especially filled with some beloved local brands, will help you imbibe the spirit of ATL. James Sung of hip Japanese spot Umi recommends purchasing tools from Cocktail Kingdom to find the quality stuff. Brendan Seery of speakeasy Himitsu warns that you should shy away from the tools that look great on a bar cart but are totally nonfunctional.

At the end of the day, it's important to have fun with it. Electric Hospitality's beverage director Timothy Parker says he has literally "shaken drinks at parties in Tupperware containers. You can church it up all you want, but at the end of the day, we're making a drink, we're trying to have something that makes you want to party a little bit. Number one is always have a little party in your heart!"

TOOLS

Cocktail shaker/shaker tin
Hawthorne strainer
Fine-mesh strainer
Julep strainer
Jigger
Mixing glass
Barspoon
Muddler
Square-ice-cube tray
Bottle opener
Bar scale
Corkscrew
Mister
Citrus peeler

GLASSWARE

Rocks glass
Double rocks glass
Nick & Nora glass
Coupe glass
Highball glass
Collins glass
Wineglass
Martini glass
Tiki glass

BITTERS, SYRUPS, MIXERS, AND OTHER INGREDIENTS

Coca-Cola

Club soda

Tonic water

Ginger beer

Pineapple juice

Orange juice

Simple syrup

18.21 Bitters

Limes

Lemons

SPIRITS

American Spirit Works Distillery Fiddler Bourbon Whiskey

American Spirit Works Distillery Resurgens Rye

Old Fourth Distillery Gin

Old Fourth Distillery Vodka

Independent Barrel Aged Rum

Independent White Rum

Hellbender Corn Whiskey

Cognac

Tequila

Mezcal

LIQUEURS

Distillery of Modern Art Peach Amaro

Blended Family Peach Liqueur

Blended Family Triple Sec No. 17

Coffee liqueur

Elderflower liqueur

Cointreau

Aperol

Little Sparrow (see pages 138–141)

How to Fit In
Like an Atlantan

Are you visiting Atlanta and trying not to stick out like a sore thumb? Here are some insider tips and tricks.

1. You can now only drink Coca-Cola products. Pepsi? Never heard of her.
2. Never pronounce the second "T" in Atlanta. It's pronounced "Atlanuh." Or after a few whiskey-and-Cokes, "Alanuh."
3. For the best experience, ask the bartender what their specialty cocktail is. Don't order a Martini at a bar best known for their bourbon.
4. If a friend suggests Johnny's Hideaway or the Clermont Lounge for a night of dancing, you should most definitely go, but not without being very, very inebriated.
5. Are you in downtown Atlanta and trying to get to a 5:30 p.m. happy hour in Buckhead? We regret to inform you that you probably should have left about three business days ago.
6. If you're not from here, get off the road. Atlanta roads are a truly godless place. Southern hospitality does not exist on I-85.
7. However, don't expect to be able to take public transportation anywhere, either. Honestly, it may be easier to just stay home.
8. Don't be surprised when a brunch out feels more like going to the club. But also, don't be surprised when the strip club is also a restaurant and a takeout wing spot.
9. Yes, explore our cocktail scene, but don't sleep on our dozens of craft breweries (Sweetwater Brewing, Scofflaw, Hippin Hops) nor our down-and-dirty dive bars (The Local, Sister Louisa's Church, Northside Tavern).

10. If you're trying to meet someone on Peachtree, make sure to check which one. We have seventy-one roads with Peachtree in the name.

11. Feel free to occasionally call Atlanta "ATL" or even "The A," but never, *ever* let the word "Hotlanta" escape your lips.

12. Be sure to head to Waffle House to fuel up after a long night of drinking and order the All-Star Special.

13. If you're out and the crowd starts chanting "ATL HOE!", simply join in and know that you're having a true ATLien experience.

Ticonderoga Club (see page 242)

BUCKHEAD:
A CROWN JEWEL

50 SHADES OF PURPLE	SO HOT RIGHT NOW
THIRSTY PHILOSOPHER	THE 13TH FLOOR
BIG TROUBLE IN OAXACA	BRAMBLE
HOLY WATER	FOUR OH FOUR
DECEPTION IN THE GARDEN	KIR DE ESPAÑA
SUN TZU	SMOKED OLD FASHIONED
HARU	TROIS MARTINI
KEMURI	GREEN LOVELACE
ALTERNATIVE MEDICINE (NA)	JUNIOR HEALY
BIJOU	MOTHER EARTH
SALTY DAWG	PUSHA TEA
OLD FASHIONED FIDDLER	POMME POMME MARTINI
THE BELLE OF THE BALL	CHOPS ESPRESSO MARTINI

One of Atlanta's most affluent areas, this northern Atlanta neighborhood is home to many luxurious shopping destinations, a plethora of corporate offices and headquarters, and a food-and-beverage scene that's long been a crown jewel in the city. Today, other intown neighborhoods are fast on the rise, and there are certainly outside-the-perimeter (OTP) destinations that are more than worth the drive. However, Buckhead continues to be a sought-after place to eat, drink, and play.

Local fun fact: If you regularly frequent the hottest Buckhead restaurants and spend most of your weekends at the luxury shopping stores in Buckhead Village or Phipps Plaza, you may get accused of being a "Buckhead Betty."

50 SHADES OF PURPLE

GYPSY KITCHEN
3035 PEACHTREE ROAD NORTHEAST SUITE A209

Gypsy Kitchen's head bartender, Ari Ghanem, wanted to create "a fun, floral, Spritz-like cocktail that evokes a sunset-by-the-sea state of mind. The novel/movie *50 Shades of Grey* was at its height of popularity and this drink also showcases a romantic ingredient like passion fruit. Furthermore, the name represents the several beautiful purple shades the cocktail gets from the butterfly pea flower infusion."

GLASSWARE: Wineglass

GARNISH: Orange slice

- 1 oz. Butterfly Pea Flower-Infused Gin (see recipe)
- 1 oz. soda water
- 1 oz. sparkling wine
- ¾ oz. Giffard Crème de Fruits de la Passion
- ¾ oz. fresh lemon juice

1. Combine all of the ingredients together in a wineglass.

2. Add ice, lightly stir, then garnish with an orange slice.

BUTTERFLY PEA FLOWER–INFUSED GIN: Let ¼ cup dried butterfly pea flowers sit in 1 liter gin for 24 hours before straining. Alternatively, you can use Empress 1908 Indigo Gin.

24 — ATLANTA COCKTAILS

THIRSTY PHILOSOPHER

KYMA

3085 PIEDMONT ROAD NORTHEAST

Kyma is a chic Greek restaurant that has been serving outstanding modern Greek food for years. The lamb filo pie? To die for! Martinis make the perfect accompaniment for Kyma's light but flavorful Mediterranean food, so it's fitting that they have a whole menu of them. The Thirsty Philosopher is a particularly hydrating take, thanks to the cucumber vodka and dill. Be sure to serve in a chilled glass for the ultimate refreshment.

GLASSWARE: Martini glass

GARNISH: Cucumber wheel, dill sprig

- 1½ oz. cucumber vodka
- ½ oz. dry gin
- ½ oz. Dill-Infused Simple Syrup (see recipe)
- ½ oz. fresh lemon juice

1. Chill a martini glass. In a cocktail shaker, combine all of the ingredients.

2. Add ice to the shaker and shake the mixture vigorously for about 10 to 15 seconds to chill the ingredients.

3. Double-strain the mixture into the chilled martini glass to remove any ice chips or herbs.

4. Garnish with a dill sprig and a cucumber wheel.

DILL-INFUSED SIMPLE SYRUP: Combine equal parts water and sugar in a saucepan. Heat until the sugar dissolves, then add fresh dill sprigs and let it simmer for a few minutes. Remove from heat, cool, and strain out the dill before using the infused syrup.

BIG TROUBLE IN OAXACA

ALMA COCINA
TERMINUS 100, 3280 PEACHTREE ROAD NORTHEAST
#100

Don't fear Midori! This lurid green liqueur sometimes gets a bad rap, but it's perfectly balanced in this drink from Ian Mendelsohn. You can also enjoy this cocktail at Alma Cocina's downtown location.

GLASSWARE: Rocks glass

- 1½ oz. Arette Blanco Tequila
- 1 oz. Pineapple Oleo (see recipe)
- ½ oz. Midori Melon Liqueur
- ½ oz. Ancho Reyes Verde Chile Liqueur
- ½ oz. fresh lemon juice

1. Add all of the ingredients to a shaker tin and shake.

2. Strain the cocktail over a single large ice cube into a rocks glass.

PINEAPPLE OLEO: After cutting the fruit from a pineapple, cut up the rind and core it into 1-inch pieces. Weigh the product and then add the same amount of white sugar to the pineapple pieces. Stir well and let the mixture sit for 2 days. Strain the juice, label it, and chill. Discard any leftover pieces.

5CHURCH

3379 PEACHTREE ROAD NORTHEAST SUITE 125

5Church is a modern American restaurant that prides itself on fresh ingredients. Their Buckhead location has a beautiful sunroom patio with walls filled with art from local Atlanta artists. Billy Turner heads up their beverage program. You can also find 5Church in Midtown, which has an excellent rooftop patio.

HOLY WATER

Perfect for the summertime, 5Church's Holy Water is a play on a Bourbon Smash. The lemon juice adds a touch of acidity to the blackberries and agave nectar, and the mint leaves add a cooling sensation.

GLASSWARE: Rocks glass

GARNISH: Blackberries, mint leaves

- **Blackberries, as needed**
- **Mint leaves, as needed**
- **1½ oz. bourbon**
- **1 oz. agave nectar**
- **¾ oz. unsweetened tea**
- **¾ oz. fresh lemon juice**

1. In a cocktail shaker, muddle the blackberries and fresh mint.
2. Add the remaining ingredients, shake with ice, and serve in a rocks glass.
3. Garnish with blackberries and mint leaves.

DECEPTION IN THE GARDEN

5CHURCH BUCKHEAD
3379 PEACHTREE ROAD NORTHEAST SUITE 125

Named after a painting of the Garden of Eden in the Buckhead location of 5Church, the Deception in the Garden is great for tequila lovers. Pineapple always pairs perfectly with tequila, and a lavender-and-pear-infused simple syrup adds a floral touch. Finally, edible flowers are a gorgeous finish.

GLASSWARE: Rocks glass

GARNISH: Dehydrated pineapple, edible flowers

- 1½ oz. Don Julio Blanco Tequila
- 1 oz. Pear Lavender Syrup (see recipe)
- ¾ oz. fresh lemon juice
- ½ oz. triple sec
- ¼ oz. pineapple juice

1. In a cocktail shaker, combine all of the ingredients with ice and shake.

2. Strain the cocktail into a rocks glass.

3. Garnish with dehydrated pineapple and edible flowers.

PEAR LAVENDER SYRUP: The pear lavender syrup, like most simple syrups, is equal parts water and sugar. De-core and dice pears, as needed. Combine the pears, water, and sugar in a pot and add dried lavender, to taste. Bring the mixture to a simmer and cook for 10 to 15 minutes. Strain the syrup, making sure to press the cooked pears to extract all their flavor. Allow the syrup to cool.

SUN TZU

5CHURCH BUCKHEAD
3379 PEACHTREE ROAD NORTHEAST SUITE 125

The light and fresh Sun Tzu was created by a gin lover on staff at 5Church. Text from *The Art of War* is painted on the ceiling of the Buckhead location of 5Church, so this drink was named Sun Tzu as a reference to that. The gin is also made by a local Atlanta distillery.

GLASSWARE: Coupe glass

GARNISH: Cucumber, mint leaves, black pepper

- Mint leaves, as needed
- 2 oz. ASW Distillery Winterville Gin
- 1 oz. cucumber water
- 1 oz. aquafaba
- ¾ oz. St-Germain Elderflower Liqueur
- ½ oz. fresh lemon juice
- ½ oz. fresh lime juice
- ½ oz. simple syrup
- Pinch salt

1. Muddle fresh mint in the bottom of a cocktail shaker.
2. Add the remaining ingredients, shake with ice, and serve straight up in a coupe.
3. Garnish with cucumber, mint, and a dash black pepper.

JAMES SUNG, UMI

Upscale Japanese restaurants are seeing an explosion in popularity in Atlanta, serving up omakase menus at increasingly eyebrow-raising prices. But even with all these newcomers excited to make their mark, Umi continues to stay at the top.

The sexy, dim lighting makes for a gorgeously moody and luxurious atmosphere. Their menu is a perfect, modern take on Japanese cuisine that will please every palate, and their omakase menu is undoubtedly one of the best in the city. Their head chef, Todd Dae Kulper, earned his stripes in the kitchens of places like French Laundry and Nobu. So it's no surprise that the same perfectionist attitudes and attention to detail can be found in Umi's beverage menu.

There are not a lot of bartenders in Atlanta who are taking the art of cocktails as seriously as Umi's James Sung is. It's impossible not to admire him for it. Unusually, he honed his craft through competitions and literature. His shelves are stocked with bar classics like *Liquid Intelligence,* and all of these efforts won him Rellies 2021 Atlanta Best Mixologist of the Year. Although he has this major accolade, James says, "The drink menu should almost be a secondary sauce for food. It should accentuate a dish, never overpower or take away from [your meal]."

Presentation is also "incredibly, incredibly, incredibly important," according to James, who adds that the lime wedges and lemons at Umi are cut "correctly," because "if you can't do the small things right, you're not going to do the big things right." Drinks should always be beautiful, and there should be care in selecting garnishes. He also wholeheartedly believes that garnishes should never get in the way of drinking your drink, so much so that James considers it a failure when a customer immediately takes out a pineapple frond garnish from a cocktail in order to drink it more easily.

One example of his perfectionism is his commitment to getting the balance of each drink not sort of right, but exactly right. One time, he worked at an ingredient for a cocktail for eight months to figure out the ratio. He fiddled with it every other day for those months, easily using "thousands of dollars" of ingredients, James estimates. But the customer, "they'll never understand that, nor should they care. The drink should just taste good, and they should love it. That first sip, you see their face change, and then they immediately go in for that second sip—that brings a lot of joy to me."

HARU

UMI
3050 PEACHTREE ROAD SUITE #1

Haru is a celebration of Japanese ingredients, and it blends beautifully together thanks to a touch of elderflower liqueur and lime juice. You can use fresh lime juice or lime super juice. Super juice reduces waste by combining fresh juice with citric acid and malic acid to make a little lime go a long way, and many people also prefer the taste.

GLASSWARE: Coupe glass

GARNISH: 2 cucumber slices

- 5 slices of cucumber
- 1 oz. gin
- 1 oz. sake
- ½ oz. shiso
- ½ oz. lime super juice
- ½ oz. St-Germain Elderflower Liqueur
- Club soda, to top

1. Muddle the cucumber slices in the bottom of a cocktail shaker.

2. Combine the remaining ingredients, except for the club soda, together in the shaker and shake with ice.

3. Double-strain the cocktail over ice into a coupe.

4. Fill the glass to the top with club soda.

5. Garnish with cucumber slices.

KEMURI

Himitsu, which means "secret" in Japanese, is one of the hottest hidden bars in town. There are several ways to get in. You can be referred by a member, make a reservation in advance, or inquire after dining at their sister restaurant, Umi, if there is any space that night at Himitsu. But now you can make their Kemuri cocktail, which means "smoke" in Japanese, anytime you'd like at home. Created by Shingo Gokan (pictured), this drink incorporates a grain whiskey made in charred American oak casks for a sweet and mellow flavor which is perfectly complemented by a smokey touch.

GLASSWARE: Snifter glass

GARNISH: Cucumber slices

- 3 to 4 cloves
- 1 oz. Nikka Coffey Grain Whisky
- ⅓ oz. oloroso sherry
- ⅓ oz. Bénédictine
- ⅓ oz. medium-dry sake
- 2 dashes aromatic bitters

1. Place the cloves on a flameproof surface and, using a butane torch, flame them and cover with a snifter glass, in the manner of a cloche.

2. Combine the remaining ingredients in a mixing glass. Add ice and stir.

3. When you have finished stirring, grab the upside-down snifter, and gently pour the cocktail through the smoke into the glass.

ALTERNATIVE MEDICINE (NA)

ROSHAMBO
2355 PEACHTREE STREET NORTHEAST

Roshambo is a modern diner in the Peachtree Battle neighborhood with a focus on comfort food and classic cocktails. It's quickly become a go-to spot for folks looking for a great meal out in an unfussy but beautiful atmosphere. Roshambo created a nonalcoholic version of the Penicillin and fittingly named it Alternative Medicine. It's both refreshing and revitalizing.

GLASSWARE: Collins glass

GARNISH: Candied ginger

- 1 oz. Square One Spicy Ginger Syrup
- 1 oz. fresh lemon juice
- ½ oz. Honey Syrup (see recipe)
- Club soda, to top

1. Build the cocktail in a shaker and double-strain it into a collins glass over fresh ice.

2. Top with club soda and garnish with a piece of candied ginger speared on a cocktail pick.

HONEY SYRUP: Combine equal parts honey and water in a saucepan over medium heat, stirring constantly. Allow the syrup to cool.

BIJOU

ROSHAMBO
2355 PEACHTREE STREET NORTHEAST

Roshambo tends to focus on classic cocktails. Bijou is a lesser-known classic drink, attributed to bartender Harry Johnson, who included the recipe in the 1900 edition of his *Bartender's Manual*. It is said to have been named for the jewel tones of its component ingredients (*bijou* is French for "jewel"). This pre-Prohibition cocktail is a mixture of gin, sweet vermouth, and Green Chartreuse—it's as if a Negroni and a Last Word found each other and created something beautiful.

GLASSWARE: Coupe glass

GARNISH: Lemon peel

- 1 oz. Hayman's London Dry Gin
- 1 oz. Green Chartreuse
- 1 oz. Cocchi Storico Vermouth di Torino

1. Chill a coupe glass.

2. Build the cocktail in a mixing glass, stir, and strain the cocktail into the chilled coupe.

3. Garnish with a lemon peel.

MADE IN GEORGIA: AMERICAN SPIRIT WORKS (ASW) DISTILLERY

199 ARMOUR DRIVE NORTHEAST C

It may be Kentucky that gets most of the shine when it comes to whiskey—you can blame our state's long-lasting holdover effects from Prohibition-era laws for that—but Georgia is quietly stepping onto the stage with its burgeoning craft distillery scene. Leading the charge is American Spirit Works Distillery, founded in 2011 by University of Georgia alumni Jim Chasteen and Charlie Thompson, and later joined by partners Justin Manglitz, Josh Anderson, Kelly Chasteen, and Chad Ralston.

It's been a stellar run of whiskey for ASW Distillery, as they have amassed quite a trove of awards and accolades in their relatively short history. Their flagship Resurgens Rye has clinched double gold medals at the prestigious San Francisco World Spirits Competition in consecutive years, while their Fiddler Bourbon range boasts its own share of silver and gold honors. Not content with just bourbon and rye, ASW has expanded its repertoire to include double malt and single malt whiskeys, including peated variations you'll usually find most often in Scotland.

Resurgens Rye, a favorite, distinguishes itself by its unique composition of 100% malted rye, resulting in a sweeter profile that sets it apart from traditional ryes. Equally beloved on Atlanta's cocktail menus is Fiddler Unison Bourbon, which blends copper-pot distilled, high-malt bourbon with foraged, high-wheat bourbon which is then aged to perfection in charred American white oak barrels.

SALTY DAWG

ASW DISTILLERY
199 ARMOUR DRIVE NORTHEAST C

While whiskey remains ASW's heart and soul, they've also ventured into crafting gin and vodka. Notably, their Hunker Vodka line should be of interest to anyone who considers themselves a Bulldogs fan. This "Vawdka" supports University of Georgia football, as opposed to Tito's, which ASW notes in their marketing materials actively supports University of Texas athletics. That alone should be reason enough to drink it! You can substitute demerara simple syrup for the jalapeño syrup.

GLASSWARE: Collins glass

GARNISH: Lime wedge

- Sea salt, for the rim
- 1½ oz. Hunker Vodka
- ¾ oz. grapefruit juice
- ¼ oz. fresh lime juice
- ¼ oz. jalapeño simple syrup
- ½ pipette 18.21 Bitters Barrel Aged Havana & Hide Bitters
- Q Mixers Sparkling Grapefruit, to top

1. Take a collins glass and use a lime wedge to wipe around the rim.
2. Dip the rim of the glass into coarse sea salt.
3. Add the remaining ingredients, except for the grapefruit soda, into a shaker with ice and shake well. Garnish with the lime wedge.

4. Strain the cocktail into the collins glass with pellet ice.

5. Fill the remainder of the glass with the soda.

6. Garnish with a lime wedge.

OLD FASHIONED FIDDLER

ASW DISTILLERY
199 ARMOUR DRIVE NORTHEAST C

If you want to enjoy a classic Old Fashioned that's truly Atlanta through and through, use ASW Distillery's Fiddler Unison Bourbon and bitters from 18.21 Bitters, as this recipe does.

GLASSWARE: Rocks glass

GARNISH: Orange peel, expressed; maraschino cherry

- **2 oz. American Spirit Works Fiddler Unison Bourbon**
- **¼ oz. demerara simple syrup**
- **1 pipette 18.21 Bitters Prohibition Bitters**
- **1 pipette 18.21 Bitters Tart Cherry & Saffron Bitters**

1. Fill a mixing glass with ice and add all of the ingredients.
2. Stir thoroughly with a barspoon, about 30 seconds.
3. Strain the cocktail into a rocks glass with a large ice cube.
4. Express an orange peel over the cocktail and add the peel as garnish, and garnish with a maraschino cherry.

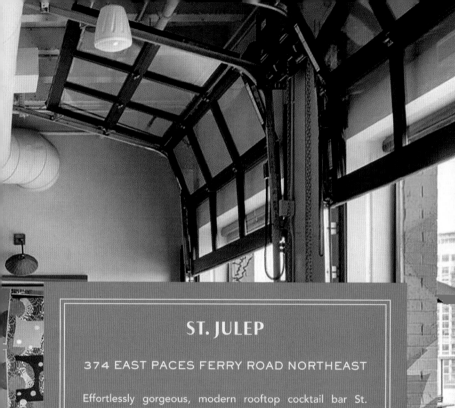

ST. JULEP

374 EAST PACES FERRY ROAD NORTHEAST

Effortlessly gorgeous, modern rooftop cocktail bar St. Julep, located atop the Kimpton Sylvan Hotel, is one of the hottest happy hour spots in Buckhead. It has a picturesque view of the city, and a selection of great drinks to boot. Their head sommelier and beverage director, Bill Brillinger, is a self-professed beverage nerd who is a certified sommelier through the court of master sommeliers and a certified bourbon professional. He loves letting his creativity run wild when creating cocktails, sometimes to the chagrin of his bartenders when he creates something too complex for them to serve in the throes of peak drink service. Visit them sometime to check it out for yourself—Brillinger is working on an Espresso Martini recipe that he is trying to make the very best in the city.

THE BELLE OF THE BALL

ST. JULEP
374 EAST PACES FERRY ROAD NORTHEAST

The Belle of the Ball is simple and clean, a great mix of Southern flavors and was created by Eric Vander Straeten.

GLASSWARE: Martini glass

GARNISH: Hibiscus flower

- 1 oz. Cathead Honeysuckle Vodka
- ½ oz. Blended Family Peach Liqueur
- ½ oz. simple syrup
- ½ oz. fresh lemon juice

1. Build the cocktail in a shaker tin with ice and shake for 15 seconds.
2. Strain the cocktail into a martini glass.
3. Garnish with a hibiscus flower.

SO HOT RIGHT NOW

ST. JULEP
374 EAST PACES FERRY ROAD NORTHEAST

E ric Vander Straeten created this fun and playful cocktail. In a city that really loves tequila, it comes as little surprise that this is St. Julep's most popular drink. Ancho Reyes Verde Chile Liqueur is a spicy, herbaceous chile liqueur, and blueberry is an unexpected but welcome touch. You can also use crushed ice if you don't have a pebble ice maker at home.

GLASSWARE: Collins glass

GARNISH: Fresh blueberries

- 1½ oz. El Jimador Reposado Tequila
- ½ oz. Blended Family Blueberry No. 22 Liqueur
- ½ oz. fresh lime juice
- ¼ oz. Ancho Reyes Verde Chile Liqueur
- 2 dashes inferno bitters

1. Build the cocktail in a shaker tin with ice and shake for 15 seconds.
2. Strain the cocktail into a collins glass and serve over pebble ice.
3. Garnish with a few fresh blueberries and stir.

THE 13TH FLOOR

An original cocktail on the St. Julep menu when it first opened, this whiskey-based drink is a mainstay.

GLASSWARE: Rocks glass

GARNISH: Orange twist

- 2½ oz. George Dickel Rye Whiskey
- ¼ oz. rich demerara syrup
- 2 dashes tiki bitters
- 2 dashes Angostura bitters

1. Build the cocktail in a mixing glass with ice.
2. Stir and strain the cocktail over a big ice cube into a rocks glass.
3. Garnish with an orange twist.

RED PHONE BOOTH

3242 PEACHTREE ROAD NORTHEAST

Red Phone Booth opened up in 2016, nearly a lifetime ago for a bar in a city as dynamic as Atlanta. Started by two industry veterans and friends, Stephen de Haan and Greg Grant, Red Phone Booth is a classic type of cigar bar with a steadfast commitment to Prohibition-era recipes. Walk into a bright-red English phone booth, dial the secret phone number, and the door opens into a sexy, cozy bar that's perfect for conversation. There's no sports TV, just Frank Sinatra music, transporting you to a bygone era. There are custom Italian leather couches

that face each other in certain areas, which encourages people to sit next to each other and meet new people.

Red Phone Both is a melting pot. It's not uncommon to find yourself rubbing elbows with your average Joe on one side, while to the other is a jet-setting multimillionaire whose passion for rare Japanese whiskeys brought him or her in.

"We acquire a lot of rare spirits, rare cigars, scotches, bourbons, and Japanese whiskeys that you cannot get anywhere else," says Greg Grant, pictured above. "But the bar program caters both to the casual drinker and the connoisseur—it's not just high-end spirits."

Eschewing the trappings of what Grant considers to be modern mixology gimmicks, Red Phone Booth prides itself on simplicity, delivering classic cocktails reminiscent of the roaring 1920s. Here, Sazeracs, Negronis, and Smoked Old Fashioneds reign supreme.

But how, then, do you have cocktails that stand out when you keep things simple and classic? Greg says that it's their bartenders, who are skilled at both their craft and conversation, and great ice. "We bring in 300-pound blocks of twice-passed, double-reverse-osmosis ice, all hand-chipped and hand-carved. It looks like a diamond; there's no air bubbles in it, no impurities. It's the purest form of ice there is. You'll have the purest form of a cocktail from the first sip to the last sip."

Premium mixers and fresh ingredients help, too. "Every juice we squeeze fresh by hand every single day. Mango, lemon, lime, cranberry, yes, even cranberry. People will get a vodka cranberry and say, 'Oh my god, it tastes bitter,' and yes, have you ever had fresh cranberries? It doesn't taste like Ocean Spray!" Greg says.

With locations in both Atlanta's downtown and Buckhead neighborhoods—as well as Dallas, Miami, Nashville, and soon, Tampa—it should be said that the downtown location is especially good for people-watching.

There was that one year at the downtown location that Atlanta hosted the Super Bowl. Red Phone Booth was bought out completely by Super Bowl sponsors and transformed into a hangout for living football legends like the Manning brothers and NFL commissioner Roger Goodell. Then there was that one night when scotch lover Joe Jonas and Jack Black wandered in while Black was in town filming *Jumanji*, sharing laughs and libations until four in the morning.

Red Phone Booth is a full-circle moment for one of its founders. Stephen de Haan's grandfather was a pharmacist at the height of Prohibition. He used to write prescriptions for "medicinal" alcohol during that era; now, his grandson honors that legacy, shaking up cocktails reminiscent of a bygone era.

BRAMBLE

The name of the drink is inspired by the shrubs, called brambles, that blackberries grow on.

GLASSWARE: Double rocks glass

GARNISH: Fresh blackberries

- 2 oz. gin
- ¾ oz. Giffard Crème de Mûre
- ¾ oz. simple syrup
- ¾ oz. fresh lemon juice

1. Combine all of the ingredients in a shaker tin with ice and shake to chill and dilute.

2. Double-strain the cocktail into a double rocks glass and garnish with fresh blackberries.

FOUR OH FOUR

RED PHONE BOOTH
3242 PEACHTREE ROAD NORTHEAST

You can probably make this refreshing and sweet drink with things you have right now at home. The number 404 is an Atlanta area code, and it's fitting that the Aperol gives this drink a bright orange color, like a Georgia peach.

GLASSWARE: Coupe glass

- 2 oz. vodka
- ¾ oz. Aperol
- ¾ oz. elderflower liqueur
- ¾ oz. fresh lemon juice

1. Chill a coupe glass. Combine all of the ingredients in a shaker tin with ice and shake to chill and dilute.

2. Double-strain the cocktail into the chilled coupe.

KIR DE ESPAÑA

RED PHONE BOOTH
3242 PEACHTREE ROAD NORTHEAST

This cocktail dates back to the nineteenth century. Grenadine and sweet vermouth add sweetness while a dash or two of Peychaud's rounds out the flavors.

GLASSWARE: Coupe glass

GARNISH: Orange peel rose, mint leaf

- **2 oz. tequila**
- **¾ oz. sweet vermouth**
- **¾ oz. grenadine**
- **2 dashes Peychaud's bitters**

1. Chill a coupe glass. Combine all of the ingredients in a shaker tin with ice and shake to chill and dilute.

2. Double-strain the cocktail into the chilled coupe and garnish with an orange peel rose and a mint leaf.

SMOKED OLD FASHIONED

RED PHONE BOOTH
3242 PEACHTREE ROAD NORTHEAST

This classic Old Fashioned is what Red Phone Booth considers its signature drink. It's a true staple that's ordered time and time again.

GLASSWARE: Double rocks glass

GARNISH: Orange peel, lemon peel, Luxardo cherry

- 2 oz. bourbon
- 1 demerara sugar cube
- 5 dashes Angostura bitters

1. Combine all of the ingredients in a mixing glass with ice and stir for 30 seconds to chill.

2. Strain the cocktail into a double rocks glass.

3. Smoke the glass using a smoke rig, butane torch, and wood chips. When smoking, always ensure the smoke rig is up out of the glass. Once you have capped the glass, wait for the smoke to settle.

4. Uncap and add a single large ice cube.

5. Garnish with an orange peel, lemon peel, and cherry.

TROIS MARTINI

Bistro Niko is an elegant French brasserie in the heart of Buckhead, an inviting place for you to immerse yourself in an enchanting environment reminiscent of Paris. The Trois Martini is Bistro Niko's crowd-pleasing take on a Martini, infused with a blend of "trois" berries—strawberries, blueberries, and raspberries. This recipe is both simple and ideal for parties. Following the directions below will create a batch of about twenty drinks. Alternatively, you can halve the recipe and store the bottle in your freezer so that this beverage is always within arm's reach.

GLASSWARE: Martini glass

GARNISH: Lemon twist

- 4 cups frozen strawberries
- 4 cups frozen blueberries
- 4 cups frozen raspberries
- 1 (1.75-liter) bottle Grey Goose Vodka
- 1 pint simple syrup, or to taste

1. Prepare a 2-gallon decanter with a secure lid. In a systematic fashion, layer frozen strawberries, frozen blueberries, and frozen raspberries within the decanter until halfway filled, allowing space for the liquor.

2. Pour the bottle of vodka into the decanter and cover with the secure lid.

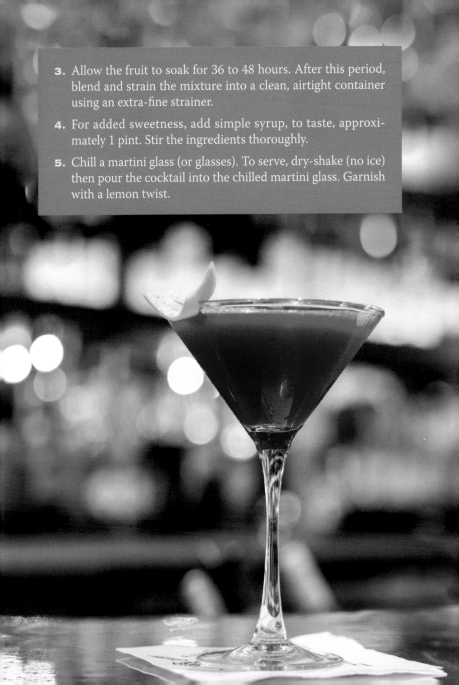

3. Allow the fruit to soak for 36 to 48 hours. After this period, blend and strain the mixture into a clean, airtight container using an extra-fine strainer.

4. For added sweetness, add simple syrup, to taste, approximately 1 pint. Stir the ingredients thoroughly.

5. Chill a martini glass (or glasses). To serve, dry-shake (no ice) then pour the cocktail into the chilled martini glass. Garnish with a lemon twist.

GREEN LOVELACE

LOCAL THREE KITCHEN & BAR
3290 NORTHSIDE PARKWAY NORTHWEST

Vodka, elderflower liqueur, and mint are a refreshing combination in this Local Three cocktail menu staple.

GLASSWARE: Rocks or martini glass

GARNISH: Mint leaf

- 2 oz. vodka
- ¾ oz. fresh lemon juice
- ½ oz. St-Germain Elderflower Liqueur
- 1 teaspoon agave nectar
- 4 mint leaves

1. Combine all of the ingredients in a cocktail shaker with ice.

2. Shake and strain the cocktail into a martini glass, or over a big cube into a rocks glass.

3. Garnish with a mint leaf.

LOCAL THREE

localthree.com

...CR 2024

KNOW. WE WANT...
...ASE LET US
...APPY AND LEAVE HAPPY
WE REALLY MEAN IT!

"CARE...

TOD...

Horseradish, Coo...

RO...
Garlic, Sn...

THE NO...
P-T...

AND OTHER THINGS SALTED...
PIG & FIG TERRINE...
FINOCCHIONA...
ORANGE FE...
NOSTR...

JUNIOR HEALY

LOCAL THREE KITCHEN & BAR
3290 NORTHSIDE PARKWAY NORTHWEST

Beverage director and partner Chris Hall estimates that Local Three easily has upwards of 1,200 varieties of whiskey, including a mind-boggling selection of 700 bourbons. The cocktail menu at Local Three changes seasonally, and it's themed based on anything from the Golden Girls to The Wire and the Wu-Tang Clan. This riff on a Manhattan has been a mainstay on Local Three's bar menu for years.

GLASSWARE: Rocks glass

GARNISH: Orange peel, expressed

- 2 oz. bourbon
- ¾ oz. ginger liqueur
- ¼ oz. blood orange liqueur
- ¼ oz. simple syrup
- 2 dashes apple bitters

1. Combine all of the ingredients in a cocktail shaker with ice and shake.

2. Double-strain the cocktail into a rocks glass over a big cube.

3. Express an orange peel segment over the drink, then add the peel as garnish.

DIN

"YOU'RE NOT JUST AN AVERAGE JOE"

TODAY'S OYSTERS

TODAY'S

"YOU CAN'T ARGUE
WITH DELICIOUS."

LOCAL
THREE

LOCALTHREE.COM

WINTER 2024

@LOCALTHREE

CHEESE

WE GOT B

CHEESE TASTING

THANDI WALTON, THOMPSON BUCKHEAD

Thandi Walton is the head of beverage for three different concepts at the Thompson Buckhead Hotel. There is Tesserae, a rooftop bar. Dirty Rascal is an old-school Italian American restaurant. Then, finally, there is Lobby Bar, a glamorous but casual hangout spot on the ground floor of the hotel.

Can you tell me a little about yourself?

I was born and raised in Africa and came to America in the late 1980s. Soon, I was part-timing in a restaurant along with going to school, and I fell in love with bartending, just watching bartenders. Coming from a British colony, my grandmother drank tea at 4 p.m. every day. I will actually rewind and say that's where my hospitality life began. When I was 8, I had to make tea for my grandmother every day, along with

scones. I had to provide the water for her to wash her hands, bring the tea, bake the scones, bring the scones for her, and then come back at the end and get the water so she could wash her hands again then collect the plates and the pots. Just caring for people, that's always been in my spirit.

I think when I said [bartending] is officially what I'm doing is when I told my mom, okay so, I'm not going back to school. I come from a long line of teachers, and I found another way where I can still actually educate by educating my guests. I told my mom I will make you proud, just let me be. And here we are!

What goes into crafting the menus at Thompson Buckhead?

It's actually kind of fun once I get past the stressful part of it! Lobby Bar is my favorite out of the three because it feels like my living room. You're in my living room, we can have cocktails and fun and no stress, you can sit with your friends and your family and chit chat and have these simple but delightful cocktails that are presented well. The presentation is always on point. But you're just chilling, so no stress.

And then you go to Dirty Rascal, okay, the Italian American thing. So now I have to incorporate two sides, I've got to have something Italian, and I've got to have something that appeals to my demographic. Most people who go to an Italian restaurant tend to lean toward wine, so how do I veer them off to drinking cocktails? And safe to say I've done a great damn job because I sell a lot of cocktails in that building! Dirty Rascal is a fun challenge because it requires me to do some research and see what riffs I can do.

Then Tesserae is very interesting because in my head I've got to do everything out of the box. I've got this cocktail now called A Trip to India and I just took all the flavors of Indian spices and made a syrup out of it. I got a Calvadore brandy, and it's amazing. There's a few things on the menu upstairs that I'd actually drink. I'm not a cocktail drinker. It's funny, I create cocktails but I don't like drinking cocktails. I taste, and I like to see people's eyes roll back, like "This is so good!" That's my satisfaction out of it.

Is there a favorite ingredient you like to incorporate into your cocktails?

I do love tea syrups. Of course, that comes from me being from Zimbabwe and drinking a lot of tea. I love making tea syrups a lot. Every menu that I have, there's going to be a tea syrup of some sort.

How important is presentation to you?

We eat with our eyes. That's a big part. Your garnish game's gotta be strong, but then sometimes the garnish can be strong and the cocktail is not balanced. So all those things tie together for me; the cocktail has to be amazing, it has to be great to complement the garnish.

Garnish-wise, I will literally look at so many things and buy so many things. I am a visual artist. I have to see it in the glass and the color of the cocktail, and I have all these garnishes in front of me, then I'll nail it every time. I just have to have a lot of options. It'll be things from the chef's cooler, then things I bought off Amazon, then things I created, dehydrating this or dehydrating that, just a combo of things. You don't have to have three garnishes on everything; I don't know who came up with that rule, but it's wack! You can have one dope garnish.

MOTHER EARTH

LOBBY BAR
415 EAST PACES FERRY ROAD NORTHEAST

Thandi Walton takes green juice and spikes it with tequila. A single pea shoot makes for a stunning garnish and fits in with Walton's "less is more" approach to garnishing.

GLASSWARE: Nick & Nora glass

GARNISH: Pea shoot

- 1 ½ oz. Tequila Herradura Reposado
- 1 oz. Green Juice (see recipe)
- ½ oz. agave nectar
- ½ oz. fresh lemon juice

1. Combine all of the ingredients in a cocktail shaker with ice and shake.

2. Strain the cocktail into a Nick & Nora.

3. Garnish with a pea shoot.

GREEN JUICE: Thandi uses a juice she calls "Green Fox Juice" that is a mix of celery, spinach, kiwi, pineapple, green apples, and lemon. You can juice up your own concoction or use your favorite green juice brand.

PUSHA TEA

Thandi Walton wanted to pay tribute to Black history and culture with her Pusha Tea cocktail, a riff on the Long Island Iced Tea, which incorporates all Black-owned spirits. Hibiscus tea also holds special significance. It originally comes from West Africa and made its way to the Americas through the Caribbean slave trade. Today, hibiscus tea is immensely popular year-round, but especially during Juneteenth celebrations as a token of remembrance for the past.

GLASSWARE: Collins glass

GARNISH: Skeleton leaf, mint leaf

- 1 oz. Peach Blossom Hibiscus Syrup (see recipe)
- ¾ oz. orange liqueur
- ¾ oz. fresh lemon juice
- ½ oz. Blackleaf Organic Vodka
- ½ oz. Bayab Classic Dry Gin
- ½ oz. Ten To One White Rum
- ½ oz. Uncle Nearest 1856

1. Chill a collins glass. Add all of the ingredients to a shaker tin with ice and shake.

2. Strain the cocktail into the collins glass.

3. Garnish with a skeleton leaf and mint leaf.

PEACH BLOSSOM HIBISCUS SYRUP: Steep 1 cup peach blossom tea and ½ cup hibiscus flowers together for at least 30 minutes. Strain the tea then combine it with an equal part sugar. Add ½ cup of Combier Crème de Pêche de Vigne.

POMME POMME MARTINI

TESSERAE
415 EAST PACES FERRY ROAD NORTHEAST

Thandi Walton takes a page out of a pastry chef's cookbook with a showstopping, abstractly shaped salted caramel tuile.

GLASSWARE: Martini glass

GARNISH: Salted Caramel Abstract Tuille (see recipe), dried flowers

- 1½ oz. Absolut Elyx Vodka
- 1½ oz. G.E. Massenez Green Apple Liqueur
- ¼ oz. Blended Family Triple Sec No. 17

1. Chill a martini glass.
2. In a mixing glass, stir all of the ingredients with ice until cold, then pour the cocktail into the chilled martini glass.
3. Garnish with a tuile and dried flowers on the stem of the glass.

SALTED CARAMEL ABSTRACT TUILLE: Add ½ cup sugar, a pinch salt, and 1½ tablespoons water to a pot, then turn the stove to medium. Stir enough to stop clumps from forming and from the sides sticking. Once it's a rich caramel color, remove the pot from heat. Take a small spoonful of caramel and drizzle it onto a sheet of parchment paper into an abstract shape. Cool to dry, then use it as a garnish. It's easier than it sounds!

CHOPS ESPRESSO MARTINI

CHOPS LOBSTER BAR
70 WEST PACES FERRY ROAD NORTHWEST

Chops is an old-school steak house with a prime selection of meat and fresh seafood flown in daily. Walk downstairs to their newly renovated Lobster Bar, a beautiful and elegant dining room with tiled arched ceilings. An espresso-flavored vodka, Kahlùa, and a shot of brewed espresso makes for an extra pleasing and extra espresso-y take on an Espresso Martini.

GLASSWARE: Martini glass

GARNISH: Coffee beans (optional)

- 1 shot espresso
- 1½ oz. Van Gogh Double Espresso Vodka
- 1 oz. Kahlúa
- ½ oz. Grand Brulot

1. Chill a martini glass. Prepare a shot of espresso and let it cool to room temperature.

2. Add a handful of ice cubes to a cocktail shaker. Pour in the vodka and liqueurs. Carefully add the cooled shot of espresso to the shaker. Seal the shaker tightly and shake the mixture vigorously for about 15 to 20 seconds to create a frothy texture.

3. Strain the shaken mixture into the chilled martini glass. Garnish with a few coffee beans, if using, on top.

WHERE TO GO FOR A BOOZY BRUNCH

Brunch is big in Atlanta, and it's not unusual to see people queuing up on any given weekend day outside of our city's best breakfast spots. These are the perfect places around town to enjoy a Mimosa along-side your meal.

BREAKFAST AT BARNEY'S
349 DECATUR STREET SOUTHEAST UNIT A1

This downtown hip eatery is about as glamorous as brunch could pos-sibly be, with green and gold touches throughout. The 24k gold pan-cakes are not only dazzling, but delicious, a little crispy on the edges and positively massive. Try the Rolls Royce cocktail, made with cognac and orange liqueur, to really booze it up.

THE BREAKFAST BOYS
3387 MAIN STREET, COLLEGE PARK

College Park has become the hot spot for some of the metro area's best brunching and more. The Breakfast Boys' catfish and grits are a revelation, as are their jerk chicken and sweet potato waffles.

JUST BRUNCH
1950 SATELLITE BOULEVARD SUITE 400, DULUTH

Chef Keith Kash cooks up some elevated brunch magic at the glamorous Just Brunch in Duluth. The Korean fried chicken cornbread waffles topped with collard greens are amazing. Try their French Espresso Martini made with Hennessy or their Banana Bread Old Fashioned to make your brunch a little more boozy.

APT. 4B
2293 PEACHTREE ROAD

This vinyl bar plus modern Caribbean restaurant serves up a killer brunch. Plantain beignets, jerk chicken omelets, and guava butter cornbread? Yes, please. The Lychee Mimosas are also perfect alongside the Caribbean fare.

LIPS ATLANTA
3011 BUFORD HIGHWAY NORTHEAST

For a drag show brunch, LIPS Atlanta is an excellent choice. Just be forewarned you may have to enjoy your French toast and Bloody Mary alongside gaggles of birthday and bachelorette parties!

MIDTOWN: ATLANTA'S HEARTBEAT

LUCKY CLOVER	CEREAL KILLER
EST OLD FASHIONED	AMOR LATINO
TERMINUS	LA LLORONA
AVANT-GARDEN	GRASSHOPPER
SOUTHERN PARADISE	NEGRONI
CHIPPED PECAN	POUSSE CAFÉ
CREOLE CREAM SODA	GÉNÉPY HIGHBALL
TUK TUK TUK	LA BOHÈME
IRISH ROSE NEGRONI	THE BEE'S GEES
FOR FIG'S SAKE!	JUNGLE BOOGIE
GUAVA LAVA MARGARITA	9-5

Midtown's skyline is impressive and ever-growing, a permanent construction zone of modern skyscrapers, each higher than the last. It's also home to one of Atlanta's greenest and most picturesque parks, Piedmont Park, which comes alive nearly every weekend with festival after festival. Art enthusiasts will love the High Museum, and Midtown is also home to a thriving gay, lesbian, and queer scene. (The city recently paid tribute to its LGTBQ community by painting a rainbow crosswalk at the intersection of 10th and Piedmont.)

Right by Georgia Tech, a premier public university known for its engineering programs, you'll find the revitalized neighborhood of West Midtown. Once a warehouse-filled industrial area, it has transformed into a haven of adaptive reuse projects for some of the city's best shopping, dining, and drinking establishments. Artists find inspiration there, renting lofts in spaces like the Goat Farm Art Center and King Plow Center. You can still spot remnants of the neighborhood's industrial history, notably the presence of railroad lines with trains still transporting goods along their tracks.

Local fun fact: Pride month was moved to October to combat the sweltering June Atlanta heat.

LUCKY CLOVER

THE ESTABLISHMENT
1197 PEACHTREE STREET NORTHEAST SUITE 517

This Clover Club riff has been a staple on The Establishment's menu for years. It's simple, fruity, and beautiful in a coupe glass.

GLASSWARE: Coupe glass

GARNISH: Dehydrated raspberry powder, dusted over the top

- 2 oz. gin
- ¾ oz. fresh lemon juice
- ¾ oz. Rosé Raspberry Cordial (see recipe)
- ¾ oz. egg white

1. Chill a coupe glass. Build the drink in a cocktail shaker and shake without ice.

2. Add ice and shake again vigorously.

3. Strain the cocktail into the chilled coupe and dust dehydrated raspberry powder over the top to garnish.

ROSÉ RASPBERRY CORDIAL: Combine 1½ cups cane sugar with 12 oz. raspberries in a ziplock bag. Let the mixture sit overnight. Add 1½ cups rosé wine and the raspberry-sugar mixture into a saucepan on low heat, stirring until the sugar is dissolved. Fine-strain but do not press the raspberry pulp.

EST OLD FASHIONED

THE ESTABLISHMENT
1197 PEACHTREE STREET NORTHEAST SUITE 517

I f you're a bar in Atlanta, you simply have to have an Old Fashioned on your menu. The Establishment swears by this one, which is made with a house-made corn oleo.

GLASSWARE: Rocks glass

GARNISH: Lemon peel, expressed; orange peel, expressed

- 2 oz. Old Grand-Dad Bottled in Bond Bourbon
- 1 teaspoon Mellow Corn Oleo (see recipe)
- 2 dashes Angostura bitters
- 2 dashes Regans' Orange Bitters No. 6
- 2 dashes Angostura orange bitters

1. Chill a rocks glass. Stir all of the ingredients in a mixing glass over ice.

2. Julep-strain the cocktail into the chilled rocks glass over ice.

3. Express a lemon peel over the top, then an orange peel. Drop both peels into drink.

MELLOW CORN OLEO: Combine 1 cup cane sugar over 4 lemon and 4 orange peels in a ziplock bag. Vacuum-seal the mixture and let it sit overnight until the sugar has absorbed the citrus oil. This is your oleo mix. Then, process 2 cups demerara sugar in a blender until it's a fine powder. Add it to a medium stockpot along with 1 cup white sugar. Add the oleo mix into the saucepot. Add 1 cup Mellow Corn and 1 cup water. Bring the saucepot to a low simmer. Do not boil! Stir until the sugars are completely dissolved. Remove from heat. Fine-strain the oleo into a container.

TERMINUS

BAR MARGOT
75 14TH STREET NORTHEAST

A trip to Bar Margot, which opened in 2015, in the Four Seasons is always an enchanting experience. Lead bartender Nick Middlebrooks named this drink, Terminus, after one of Atlanta's original names. He wanted to create a drink representative of Georgia, and he certainly achieved that with rye whiskey, chicory bitters, pecan liqueur, and a spray of pipe tobacco. Vermouth adds some balance to this spirit-forward drink.

GLASSWARE: Nick & Nora glass

GARNISH: Atomized Pipe Tobacco (see recipe), flamed orange expression

- 1½ oz. Rittenhouse Straight Rye Whiskey
- ½ oz. Cocchi Storico Vermouth di Torino
- ½ oz. Rivulet Artisan Pecan Liqueur
- ¼ oz. Bénédictine
- 2 dashes Angostura bitters
- 2 dashes El Guapo Chicory Pecan Bitters

1. Combine all of the ingredients in a shaker tin with water, shake, then double-strain the cocktail into a Nick & Nora.

2. Garnish with Atomized Pipe Tobacco and a flamed orange expression.

ATOMIZED PIPE TOBACCO: Steep 200 grams Q1 pipe tobacco in 1 quart water. Strain the infusion, then add it to an atomizer.

AVANT-GARDEN

BAR MARGOT
75 14TH STREET NORTHEAST

The Avant-Garden is a play on a Spritz by Nick Middlebrooks. It's a little different than an Aperol or Hugo Spritz—there's floral and sweetness from the St-Germain, but then additional herbaceousness that comes through from the house-made cucumber syrup. Hibiscus tea not only tastes amazing but adds a brilliant color.

GLASSWARE: Wineglass

GARNISH: Cucumber wrap, hibiscus flower, rosemary sprig

- 2 oz. Cucumber Hibiscus Syrup (see recipe)
- 1 oz. St-Germain Elderflower Liqueur
- ¾ oz. fresh lime juice
- 4 oz. Lucien Sparkling Rosé, to top

1. Add a cucumber wrap to a wineglass.

2. Combine all of the ingredients in the glass, filling to the top with rosé.

3. Garnish with a hibiscus flower and rosemary sprig.

CUCUMBER HIBISCUS SYRUP: Chop 1 cucumber into coins and add salt. Let them rest for 30 minutes while making hibiscus tea (1 cup hibiscus to 4 cups water). Then add 2 cups sugar. Blend the cucumbers thoroughly and add them to the hibiscus tea. Strain out the cucumber and hibiscus bits.

SOUTHERN PARADISE

BAR MARGOT
75 14TH STREET NORTHEAST

The Southern Paradise is Middlebrooks's play on a Gin Fizz. He wanted to have something tropical on Bar Margot's winter menu and was able to use passion fruit liqueur which is easy to obtain year-round.

GLASSWARE: Coupe glass

GARNISH: Sage leaf, angostura spray

- 1¼ oz. Bulrush Gin
- 1 oz. Banana Oat Vanilla Syrup (see recipe)
- 1 oz. fresh lemon juice
- 1 egg white
- ½ oz. Chinola Passionfruit Liqueur

1. Combine all of the ingredients in a shaker tin, shake, then add ice and shake again.

2. Garnish with a spray of angostura bitters from a mister and a sage leaf.

BANANA OAT VANILLA SYRUP: Heat up 4 cups oat milk, then add 4 cups sugar and 4 chopped bananas. Blend thoroughly in a blender, strain, and add 1 tablespoon vanilla bean paste.

CHIPPED PECAN

SOUTH CITY KITCHEN
1144 CRESCENT AVENUE NORTHEAST

A pecan-infused molasses makes South City Kitchen's Old Fashioned decidedly Southern.

GLASSWARE: Rocks glass

GARNISH: Orange peel, expressed

- 2 oz. Shortbarrel Rye 101
- 1 teaspoon Fernet-Branca
- 2 teaspoons Pecan-Infused Blackstrap Molasses (see recipe)

1. Add all of the ingredients to a shaker. Add ice and stir for 15 seconds.

2. Double-strain the cocktail into a rocks glass with a large ice cube. Express an orange peel over the cocktail, then add the peel as a garnish.

PECAN-INFUSED BLACKSTRAP MOLASSES: Toast 1 cup pecans either in the oven or a pan until just toasted. Add 1 cup water and 1 cup molasses into a pot. Heat and stir until the mixture reaches a simmer. Turn off the heat and add the toasted pecans. Let the mixture infuse overnight. Double-strain and chill.

THE CONSULATE

10 10TH STREET NORTHWEST SUITE P200

Every ninety days, popular Midtown restaurant The Consulate changes over its menu to feature cuisine from a new country in the world. At their "spin parties," one lucky patron literally spins a globe, and wherever their finger lands becomes the country that will inspire an entirely new seasonal menu. With that, new cocktails, too. Their beverage director, Walter Gregg, takes these opportunities to research and try out new liqueurs and flavors from the chosen region. So far, he's created around thirty-five different libations for the restaurant's various concepts.

CREOLE CREAM SODA

The Creole Cream Soda was a Walter Gregg concoction that could be enjoyed alongside The Consulate's recent menu featuring delicacies from Papua New Guinea. The Creole Cream Soda is a supremely sippable, crowd-pleasing mix of rum, vanilla, and heavy whipping cream, sweet with just a touch of frothiness.

GLASSWARE: Mason jar

- 1½ oz. dark rum
- ½ oz. 151 overproof rum
- ½ oz. vanilla liqueur
- ½ oz. simple syrup
- ¼ oz. fresh lemon juice
- ¼ oz. heavy whipping cream
- Ginger ale, to top

1. Combine all of the ingredients in a shaker tin and shake well with ice.
2. Pour the ingredients into a mason jar glass and add ginger ale until you fill to the top.

THE SECRET WORLD OF 007

RAVEL BOOK

TUK TUK TUK

THE CONSULATE
10 10TH STREET NORTHWEST SUITE P200

The Tuk Tuk Tuk, named as a reference to the "tuk tuk tuk" sound that the rickshaws make across Southeast Asia, is a boozy, cognac-based drink that gets a tropical touch with pineapple amaro and a half ounce of lemon juice. The drink was featured on The Consulate's Cambodian menu—a nice complement to some of the tropical Cambodian flavors.

GLASSWARE: Coupe glass

GARNISH: Lemon peel

- 1 oz. cognac
- ¾ oz. Heirloom Pineapple Amaro
- ¾ oz. Pasubio Vino Amaro
- ½ oz. fresh lemon juice
- 2 dashes Peychaud's bitters

1. Combine all of the ingredients in a cocktail shaker and shake well with ice.

2. Double-strain the cocktail into a coupe and garnish with a lemon peel.

IRISH ROSE NEGRONI

THE CONSULATE
IO IOTH STREET NORTHWEST SUITE P200

Amaro offsets the sweetness of the strawberry-infused gin and exquisite Brovo Pink Vermouth for a perfectly balanced twist on a Negroni. It's simply fabulous. This Negroni is sweet, but not in a cloying way, and it still has the delightful booziness of a Negroni. The Irish Rose Negroni was featured on The Consulate's Ireland menu and pays homage to Ireland's roses—a symbol less renowned than the shamrock but still culturally significant to the Emerald Isle.

GLASSWARE: Rocks glass

GARNISH: Strawberry slice

- 1 oz. Strawberry-Infused Gin (see recipe)
- 1 oz. Rockey's Milk Punch
- ½ oz. BROVO Pink Rosé Vermouth
- ½ oz. Lo-Fi Gentian Amaro

1. Combine all of the ingredients in a mixing glass and stir 40 rotations.

2. Pour the cocktail into a rocks glass over 1 big cube. Garnish with a slice of strawberry.

STRAWBERRY-INFUSED GIN: Take about ½ cup cut strawberries and mix them into 1 (1-liter) bottle of Glendalough Rose Gin, seal the bottle, shake, then let it sit in your refrigerator for at least 24 hours. Strain before using.

DRAWBAR

1 INTERLOCK AVENUE NORTHWEST

Hotel bars aren't just for tourists anymore. Drawbar is a beautiful terrace bar in West Midtown with a dramatic view of Atlanta's skyline, and food and beverage manager Daniel Torres says its clientele are actually mostly locals looking to unwind after work or in search of a lively night out. Daniel loves to experiment with his drink menu, and a new program they're working on will incorporate flavors from seafood, like caviar and the saltiness of sardines. Another fun fact is that Drawbar's name is a nod to West Midtown's railway past. A "drawbar" is the term for the metal bar that connects two railroad cars, and Drawbar seeks to be a connecting point for people. "It's almost like a living room; we want to draw you in, get you in, and make you feel comfortable."

FOR FIG'S SAKE!

DRAWBAR
I INTERLOCK AVENUE NORTHWEST

A popular cocktail at Drawbar, Daniel Torres says his For Fig's Sake! is a "winter-going-into-spring moment." Use freshly squeezed lemon juice for the best results. For the syrup, you can also try to create your own at home.

GLASSWARE: Collins glass
GARNISH: Fresh fig half

- 2 oz. Tito's Handmade Vodka
- ¾ oz. Liber & Co. Caramelized Fig Syrup
- ¾ oz. fresh lemon juice
- Ginger beer, to top

1. Place all of the ingredients, except for the ginger beer, in a cocktail shaker with ice.

2. Pour the cocktail into a collins glass and top it off with ginger beer.

GUAVA LAVA MARGARITA

DRAWBAR

I INTERLOCK AVENUE NORTHWEST

Try saying "Guava Lava Margarita" five times fast, especially after having a few of them. Guava, jalapeño, and pumpkin make the perfect match in this Margarita. It's sweet, smoky, and gorgeous in your glass. It's a perfectly balanced take on a Margarita, and so deliciously fragrant! On a recent night out with work, I ordered one of these, which caused my coworker to look around the room and ask, "Who ordered jalapeño poppers?"

GLASSWARE: Rocks glass

GARNISH: Dehydrated lime

- 2 oz. Tanteo Jalapeño Tequila
- 1 oz. fresh lime juice
- ½ oz. guava syrup
- ½ oz. pumpkin syrup

1. Place all of the ingredients in a shaker with ice. Shake, then pour the cocktail into a rocks glass.

2. Top with a dehydrated lime.

CEREAL KILLER

You can't accuse Drawbar of not having fun when they literally infuse Maker's Mark with cereal marshmallows. Let your inner child sing with this drink!

GLASSWARE: Coupe glass

GARNISH: Cereal marshmallows

- 2 oz. Marshmallow-Infused Bourbon (see recipe)
- 1 oz. fresh lemon juice
- 1 oz. simple syrup
- 1 egg white

1. Combine all of the ingredients in a cocktail shaker and dry-shake.

2. Pour the cocktail into a coupe.

MARSHMALLOW-INFUSED BOURBON: Mix 1 (750 ml) bottle of Maker's Mark with 1 cup cereal marshmallows. Infuse for 24 to 48 hours in an airtight bottle in your refrigerator, strain, then rebottle.

ALTATORO

33 PEACHTREE PLACE NORTHEAST

AltaToro is a show and a restaurant in one, featuring flavors from all over Latin America and, most nights, fire-breathing dancers! Their beverage menu features Latin American classic cocktails with a twist.

AMOR LATINO

ALTATORO
33 PEACHTREE PLACE NORTHEAST

Tequila is very much like wine: it's very terroir driven, where the area and production process greatly changes the flavor," says AltaToro's beverage director, Billy Turner. He also loves to use tropical flavors like passion fruit and mango on the menu at AltaToro. The Amor Latino is a popular drink, a play on the Capeta that's popular in Brazil. He swaps out coconut milk for coconut water so the drink is extra refreshing.

GLASSWARE: Rocks glass

GARNISH: Lime wheel, toasted coconut shavings

- Tajín, for the rim
- 2 oz. Corazon Tequila
- 1 oz. Passion Fruit Simple Syrup (see recipe)
- 1 oz. pineapple juice
- 1 oz. coconut water
- ½ oz. coconut rum
- ½ oz. fresh lime juice

1. Wet the rim of a rocks glass then dip it into Tajín to give it a rim.

2. Shake all of the ingredients in a cocktail shaker with ice and serve the cocktail in a rocks glass.

3. Garnish with a lime wheel and toasted coconut shavings.

PASSION FRUIT SIMPLE SYRUP: Combine equal parts water, sugar, and passion fruit puree in a pot over medium heat. Heat until the sugar is dissolved and everything is blended. Allow the syrup to cool then strain.

LA LLORONA

Mezcal brings smokiness, Aperol adds bitterness, and génépy brings in rosemary, thyme, and licorice root flavors to this drink. La Llorona is named after the legend of a ghost in Latin America who was said to roam near bodies of water, mourning her children who she drowned in a rage after her husband left her. A little dark, so be careful with this one!

GLASSWARE: Coupe glass

GARNISH: Carved lemon peel

- ¾ oz. Mezcal Illegal
- ¾ oz. Dolin Génépy
- ¾ oz. Aperol
- ¾ oz. fresh lemon juice

1. Shake all of the ingredients in a cocktail shaker with ice then strain the cocktail into a coupe.

2. Garnish with a carved lemon peel.

ALLISON LOVELACE, BAR BLANC

A sexy new addition has arrived fresh on the bar scene in Atlanta. Bar Blanc is a glamorous ode to Paris. It is both a bar and steak friterie, with just one thing on the food menu: a prix-fixe meal consisting of a mixed greens salad, crusty bread, steak served in a cast-iron skillet with a side of brown butter bearnaise sauce, and unlimited thick-cut fries. Downstairs sits Little Sparrow, a full-service French brasserie that's an ode to Edith Piaf.

Allison Lovelace, who has worked in the food and beverage industry for fifteen years now, manages the bar programs at both concepts, along with the upscale steakhouse, Marcel.

For Allison, bartending is a chance for her to unleash a creative side since she says she "grew up not super creative. When I started making cocktails, I realized there was a part of my brain I had never used until that moment."

For Bar Blanc, she goes the classic cocktail route and seeks out simplicity. For Little Sparrow, she incorporates a little more creativity, but for both concepts she focuses on using "really high-quality spirits, where the distiller and the farmer are doing things the correct way. I'd rather spend more money on the product and have a better version of it than go the affordable route and make something mediocre," she says. "I come from a very large Italian and French Catholic family. A lot of things are built around eating and drinking. Almost every night at the restaurant, it's a very special thing—it's almost like I'm hosting a dinner party every night."

For the at-home bartender trying to level up their game, Allison has some sage advice: Work on your technique, and make sure your drinks have proper dilution. When a drink is too tart or too sweet, it likely can benefit from a little extra water gained from just a few seconds longer in the shaker.

"Shaking can be uncomfortable; you almost *never* look cool doing it in the beginning," Allison says with a laugh. "Your whole body is shaking when you're shaking cocktails for people; you kind of want that whole process to be over as quickly as possible. It's something I always tell my mom and my sister: literally just shake it a couple seconds longer than you think you need to shake it, and it's going to be what you're looking for!"

GRASSHOPPER

BAR BLANC
1198 HOWELL MILL ROAD

This classic cream-based drink, which is usually a lurid green color from crème de menthe, was a huge hit in days of yesteryear. Beverage director Allison Lovelace makes it cool and modern with her take on it, which uses a mint liqueur and cacao liqueur. She uses a Japanese bitters bottle for more precision with her bitters. This way, a dash is always a dash, which tends to be a problem with other bottles.

GLASSWARE: Nick & Nora glass

GARNISH: Mint leaf

- ¾ oz. heavy cream
- ¾ oz. Bordiga Centum Herbis
- ½ oz. Tempus Fugit Crème de Cacao
- ½ oz. vodka
- ¼ oz. Giffard Menthe-Pastille
- 6 dashes Bittermen's Xocolatl Mole Bitters

1. Combine all of the ingredients in a mixing tin, add ice, and shake.
2. Double-strain the cocktail into a Nick & Nora.

NEGRONI

BAR BLANC
1198 HOWELL MILL ROAD

The Negroni may be an Italian invention, but a touch of American-made aperitivo fits perfectly well here in Bar Blanc's simple take.

GLASSWARE: Rocks glass

GARNISH: Orange twist, stamped ice cube

- **1 oz. Murrell's Row GinGin**
- **1 oz. House Vermouth (1:1 Lustau Vermut Rojo and Bordiga Vermouth Rosso)**
- **½ oz. Campari**
- **¼ oz. Forthave RED Aperitivo**

1. Combine all of the ingredients in a mixing glass with ice. Stir and strain the cocktail over a stamped iceberg in a rocks glass.

2. Garnish with an orange twist.

POUSSE CAFÉ

It's impossible to resist the beauty of a colorful, layered drink. A Pousse Café, which is French for "push the coffee," is generally an after-dinner and coffee drink. Pour the heaviest liquid first, then the least dense on top. Serve it in a clear glass to see all the layers.

GLASSWARE: Cordial glass

- ½ oz. Jules Theuriet Crème de Cassis
- ½ oz. Bordiga Maraschino
- ½ oz. Campari

- ½ oz. Bordiga Centum Herbis
- ½ oz. Spirulina Fino Sherry
- ½ oz. Dudognon Seleccion

1. Carefully layer the ingredients in a cordial glass, beginning with the cassis and ending with the Dudognon Seleccion. Pour each layer in using the end of a barspoon to create a layered effect.

GÉNÉPY HIGHBALL

LITTLE SPARROW
1198 HOWELL MILL ROAD

The Génépy Highball is made with a complicated house-made tonic syrup that's tart and zesty with lemongrass in it, but they recommend at home you use Jack Rudy's tonic syrup, since making tonic syrup at home can sometimes be dangerous if you use too much chincona bark. Génépy adds even more botanical elements to Beefeater Gin, a gin that has been in production since 1876 characterized by juniper and other notes like angelica root, coriander seeds, and Seville oranges.

GLASSWARE: Collins glass
GARNISH: 2 lime wheels, lime zest

- 1 oz. Montane Original Sparkling Water
- ¾ oz. Jack Rudy Cocktail Co. Classic Tonic Syrup
- ¾ oz. Beefeater Gin
- ½ oz. Alpe Génépy

1. Build the drink in a collins glass: add the sparkling water to the glass, then add the rest of the ingredients, then garnish with 2 lime wheels on the side of the glass.

2. Add an ice spear and top with more sparkling water.

3. Channel lime zest over the top.

LA BOHÈME

LITTLE SPARROW
1198 HOWELL MILL ROAD

Rye gets extra flavor in this cocktail at Little Sparrow. A French herbal liqueur, Bénédictine, and Royal Combier Grand Liqueur, a cognac-based liqueur, combine for a spirit-forward drink. A few dishes of chocolate bitters are a genius finishing touch.

GLASSWARE: Coupe glass

GARNISH: Dehydrated lemon wheel

- 1¼ oz. PM Spirits Overproof Armagnac
- ½ oz. Bordiga Extra Dry Vermouth
- ½ oz. Rittenhouse Straight Rye Whiskey
- ¼ oz. Bénédictine
- ¼ oz. Royal Combier Grand Liqueur
- 4 dashes Angostura bitters
- 8 dashes Bittermens Xocolatl Mole Bitters

1. Combine all of the ingredients in a mixing glass with ice, stir, and strain the cocktail into a coupe.

2. Garnish with a dehydrated lemon wheel.

JOJO'S BELOVED

1197 PEACHTREE STREET NORTHEAST

JoJo's Beloved channels everything cool from the disco era in a sultry, inviting cocktail lounge. Nestled in the back corner of the upscale Politan Row food hall, JoJo's Beloved is a fully immersive experience incorporating the best of the 1970s and the 1980s. An all-vinyl soundtrack sets the mood, featuring legends of yesteryear like Diana Ross, David Bowie, and Prince. In the center of the space, there's a feminine, pink-marble, U-shaped bar, beckoning its guests to engage in lively conversation and mingle. Luxurious touches abound with lush velvet drapes, glamorous brassy golds, neon accents, rich red hues, and plush plaid booths, perfect for relaxed lounging and intimate conversations.

For anyone who remembers cocktails during these decades, you can probably acknowledge that despite being very fun, "They weren't very great," says Qwesha Byrd. "It was a lot of sour mix and a lot of sweet drinks, not a lot of caretaking in place for cocktails of that era. So our thing was, taking that cocktail that people may not think is so crafty, how can we elevate it? How can we make it crafty?"

Determined to elevate these classics, JoJo's Beloved has reimagined throwback drinks like White Russians and ingredients like Midori, presenting them in a tastefully modern, balanced manner. Byrd says the menu often evokes nostalgic reactions from older guests, who will say, "This is something that I never thought I'd get to drink again." It goes to show how well JoJo's Beloved really hits that era's mark.

A recent exciting development for both JoJo's Beloved and Atlanta is they have now expanded their back room. Their dance floor is just as seductive as their front lounge, and it's pumping disco tunes on the weekends. Unlike their lounge, you don't need a reservation to visit the back bar. They've dubbed this dance floor the Roselight Room as an homage to Atlanta's legendary Limelight club. It's certainly a place where you can lose yourself in the glitz of a bygone era, all under the shimmering glow of a disco ball.

THE BEE'S GEES

JOJO'S BELOVED
1197 PEACHTREE STREET NORTHEAST

Some recipes just write themselves. In an attempt to update the classic Sloe Gin Fizz, it became obvious to Sophie Burton and Benton Bourgeois at JoJo's Beloved to marry it with gin classics of other eras. This contemporary version of the Sloe Gin Fizz borrows from the honey-laced Bee's Knees, and the bubbly French 75. It's been on JoJo's menu since the beginning, and will probably never leave. The color even matches the decorations at JoJo's!

GLASSWARE: Coupe glass

GARNISH: Dehydrated lemon

- ½ oz. fresh lemon juice
- ½ oz. honey syrup
- ½ oz. Hayman's Sloe Gin
- ½ oz. Cadão Ruby Port
- ½ oz. Galliano Autentico
- 2 oz. sparkling wine, to top

1. Chill a coupe glass. Combine all of the ingredients, except for the sparkling wine, in a shaker tin and add ice. Shake until cold.

2. Fine-strain the cocktail into the chilled coupe.

3. Top with your favorite sparkling wine. Garnish with a dehydrated lemon.

JUNGLE BOOGIE

JOJO'S BELOVED
1197 PEACHTREE STREET NORTHEAST

The Jungle Boogie was created as a love letter to the creator's favorite tropical cocktail, the Jungle Bird. Jamaican rums are swapped with a blend of Havana Club and Clairin, a Haitian rum made from sugarcane juice and wild yeast. The end result is a cocktail that Qwesha Byrd says hits all the notes—a little sweet, a little tart, and a little boozy.

GLASSWARE: Rocks glass

GARNISH: Dehydrated pineapple slice, 2 pineapple fronds

- 1½ oz. fresh pineapple juice
- ¾ oz. **Havana Club Añejo Blanco**
- ¾ oz. **Spirit of Haiti Clairin Communal**
- ½ oz. fresh lime juice
- ½ oz. simple syrup
- ½ oz. **Luxardo Bitter Bianco**

1. Add all of the ingredients to a cocktail shaker and add ice.

2. Shake hard, then strain the cocktail over fresh cubes into a rocks glass.

3. Garnish with 2 pineapple fronds and a dehydrated pineapple slice.

JOJO'S BELOVED
1197 PEACHTREE STREET NORTHEAST

Before Dick Bradsell made his first Espresso Martini, there was the Black Russian. Gabriel Jaramillo's version combines the two and adds coconut rum and blackstrap molasses for a richer and slightly tropical twist. To make it a White Russian, he combines coconut milk, vanilla liqueur, and a little simple syrup.

GLASSWARE: Rocks glass

GARNISH: Coconut Foam (see recipe), espresso powder

- 1 oz. Wheatley Vodka
- 1 oz. Don Q Coco
- 1 oz. Cold Brew Concentrate (see recipe)
- ½ oz. St. George NOLA Coffee Liqueur
- ¼ oz. blackstrap molasses syrup

1. Add all of the ingredients to a rocks glass with ice. Stir until chilled.

2. Garnish with the foam and espresso powder.

COCONUT FOAM: An iSi whipper and Whip-Its! NO₂ cartridges are needed for home mixologists interested in making a foam as airy as Gabriel's. Take 12 oz. coconut milk, 6 oz. Giffard Vanille de Madagascar, and 6 barspoons simple syrup, and add them to a 750 ml iSi whipped cream dispenser. Charge the dispenser with 1 cartridge, shake, and serve. Best if the ingredients are cold.

COLD BREW CONCENTRATE: Using a steeping bag, place 4 oz. coarse-ground coffee in a mason jar. Pour 16 oz. cold, filtered water into the jar and seal the jar. Allow the concentrate to steep for 18 hours. Remove the coffee grounds before use.

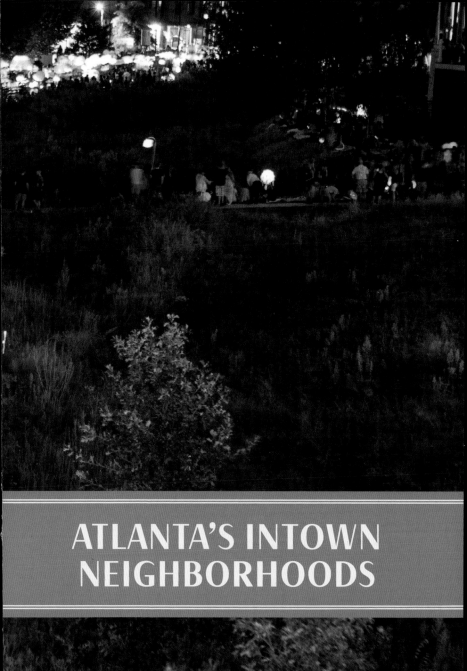

ATLANTA'S INTOWN
NEIGHBORHOODS

CHICHA SOUR	CRETAN BULL
CHILCANO	ROYAL GROVE
PISCO SOUR	3 STACKS
TAMARIND CAIPIRINHA	HONEY HIBISCUS PALOMA
DECATUR DAIQUIRI	RED MOON OVER MANHATTAN
RADISH ME THIS	WARM WINTER
CAFÉ ON COLLEGE	THE VESPER
LEMON PEPPER WET	DAMIEN'S MANHATTAN
WIDOW MAKER	STATELY HAG
THE FERRYMAN	CARELESS WHISPER #2
SLEEPLESS IN SEATTLE	LEXINGTON LAYOVER
FRENCH 75	BLACKEST HEART
APPLETINI	A LEAVE OF ABSINTHE
DUBOIS DAQUIRI	LA BEFANA
TOASTED OLD FASHIONED	DR. NEMESIS
ATL STREET SOUR	NEGRONI
SUMMER TONIC	

Midtown and Buckhead may form the industrial heart of Atlanta, but it's Atlanta's distinct intown neighborhoods that hold the city's charm. Atlanta is a city chock-full of neighborhoods—242, to be exact—so you'll have to forgive me for crudely lumping them together for the purposes of organizing this book.

The truth is, each neighborhood has its own personality and distinct flavor. Decatur holds some of the city's best dining and drinking, while eclectic East Atlanta is where many of our city's artists and creatives call home. Virginia-Highlands offers a delightful mix of historic restaurants and taverns as well as a rambunctious nightlife. The Grant Park neighborhood is steeped in history, home to Zoo Atlanta and the Atlanta Cyclorama, and its park is one of the city's most beautiful.

Local fun fact: Old Fourth Ward is where you can find the boyhood home of Martin Luther King Jr.

CHICHA SOUR

TIO LUCHO'S
675 NORTH HIGHLAND AVENUE NORTHEAST
SUITE 6000

Chef Arnaldo Castillo's Tio Lucho's is currently the only purely Peruvian restaurant in the city of Atlanta, but we certainly hope it won't be ATL's last. The menu features mind-bogglingly good food that even nabbed the chef a nomination for Best Chef in the Southeast by the James Beard Foundation. On Tio Lucho's drink menu, the Peruvian national spirit, pisco, takes center stage. A half ounce of Chicha Morada makes this simple drink a gorgeous one.

GLASSWARE: Pisco glass
GARNISH: Lime wheel

- 1½ oz. pisco
- ¾ oz. egg white
- ¾ oz. fresh lime juice
- ½ oz. clove simple syrup
- ½ oz. chicha morada

1. Pour all of the ingredients into a cocktail shaker and dry-shake.
2. Add ice and shake again.
3. Pour the cocktail into a pisco glass.
4. Garnish with a lime wheel.

CHILCANO

TIO LUCHO'S
675 NORTH HIGHLAND AVENUE NORTHEAST
SUITE 6000

Chef Arnaldo Castillo wanted to have a drink on the menu that's approachable for diners who may be wary of things like egg whites in cocktails. The Chilcano is not as widely known as say, the Pisco Sour, but Arnaldo has fond memories of enjoying it while in Peru as a teenager with his cousins, with ginger ale, a can of peaches, and pisco. In the summer months, Arnaldo switches up the Chilcano and will create syrups to make it even more flavorful, but here's how to make a basic one for now.

GLASSWARE: Tin mug

GARNISH: Lime wedge

- 2 oz. pisco
- ¼ oz. fresh lime juice
- Ginger ale, to top

1. Combine the pisco, lime juice, and lime wedge in a tin mug.
2. Top with ginger ale.

PISCO SOUR

TIO LUCHO'S
675 NORTH HIGHLAND AVENUE NORTHEAST
SUITE 6000

Pisco is "Peruvian, not Chilean," says Arnaldo Castillo, so don't get it wrong. The Pisco Sour is the most common drink you'll find incorporating this spirit. Tio Lucho's likes to use Barsol Quebranta for their pisco, but you can use whichever brand you'd like.

GLASSWARE: Pisco glass

GARNISH: Peruvian flag made from a Peychaud's bitters mist split with a toothpick

- 1½ oz. Barsol Quebranta Pisco
- ¾ oz. egg white
- ¾ oz. fresh lime juice
- ½ oz. simple syrup
- ½ oz. apricot liqueur

1. Pour all of the ingredients into a cocktail shaker and dry-shake.

2. Add ice and shake again.

3. Pour the cocktail into a pisco glass and garnish with a Peruvian flag.

TAMARIND CAIPIRINHA

TIO LUCHO'S
675 NORTH HIGHLAND AVENUE NORTHEAST
SUITE 6000

W hen they're not using pisco, Tio Lucho's seeks to highlight other iconic Latin American drinks. Tamarind adds a bit of flare to a classic Brazilian Caipirinha.

GLASSWARE: Rocks glass

GARNISH: Lime wedge

- **2 oz. tamarindo**
- **1½ oz. cachaça**
- **¼ oz. fresh lime juice**

1. Pour all of the ingredients into a cocktail shaker with ice and shake hard.
2. Dirty-dump the cocktail into a rocks glass and garnish with a lime wedge.

INDEPENDENT DISTILLING COMPANY

547 EAST COLLEGE AVENUE, DECATUR

Founder Michael Anderson had a long career in nonprofit fundraising before teaming up with experienced Atlanta barman Casey Teague to form Independent Distilling Company.

While their inaugural product, Hellbender Corn Whiskey, marked their debut, this Decatur-based distillery has since broadened its repertoire to include bourbon, rye, white rum, and barrel-aged rum.

Independent is the perfect name for this distillery, because it certainly feels very DIY, albeit in the most charming way. The outside of their building is totally nondescript and easy to miss. In their tasting room, simple paper decorations adorn the ceilings, repurposed barrels are the tables, and much of the furniture looks like it was just picked up at the thrift store.

That's not to say that their products are not quality, however. Independent Distilling Company uses a one-hundred-gallon copper pot still to craft its spirits. Their Hellbender Straight Rye Whiskey uses locally sourced rye that is ground then blended with malted wheat for a long fermentation. It's then aged in new charred American white oak to create a true Georgia product.

Independent Distilling is one of the few rum creators in Georgia. Inspired by the great spirits at Georgia's Richland Rum Distillery, Anderson wanted to create his own take on rum. Their barrel-aged rum stands apart from most rum on the market since it uses table grade, rather than blackstrap, molasses. This creates a full-bodied rum that was voted Best Georgia Distilled Spirit in the Georgia Trustees Wine and Spirits Competition.

Barman Casey Teague is throwing it down with the cocktail menu in their tasting room. He is constantly exploring new frontiers when it comes to drink creation and using garnishes and ingredients grown in their herb garden. For example, on the distillery's most recent cocktail menu, there is a rum-based drink that incorporates, among other ingredients, goat's milk, Coca-Cola, duck egg, and Parmesan—simply because he wanted to incorporate as many different animals as possible in a drink and see how and if they could work together.

You'll also see their independent spirit in a lot of one-off partnerships they do, like a spirit they're calling Bierschnapps that they fermented out of a bad batch of beer from their neighboring brewery, Three Taverns Craft Brewery. Where some may ask why, Independent Distilling asks, Why not? And Atlanta is better for it.

DECATUR DAIQUIRI

INDEPENDENT DISTILLING
547 EAST COLLEGE AVENUE, DECATUR

A house-made lemongrass syrup makes this classic Daiquiri extra delicious.

GLASSWARE: Hurricane glass

GARNISH: Umbrella, lime wheel

- 2 oz. Independent White Rum
- ¾ oz. fresh lime juice
- ¾ oz. Lemongrass Syrup (see recipe)
- Dash Regans' Orange Bitters No. 6
- ½ oz. fresh cane juice (optional), to top

1. Add all of the ingredients, except for the cane juice, to a shaker with ice and shake.

2. Strain the cocktail into a hurricane glass and garnish with a lime wheel and umbrella.

3. If you can obtain it, Teague also recommends adding ½ oz. fresh cane juice to bring out the grassy notes in the rum.

LEMONGRASS SYRUP: Take 1 cup chopped lemongrass, 1 cup sugar, and 1 cup freshly brewed coffee and add them into a blender. Blend on high until the sugar is dissolved. Let the syrup macerate overnight, then strain out the lemongrass chunks.

RADISH ME THIS

INDEPENDENT DISTILLING
547 EAST COLLEGE AVENUE, DECATUR

Casey Teague takes a "more is more" approach to a Gin and Tonic, which is how he likes to enjoy them while relaxing at home. It's a garden in a cup, and so fragrant and delicious!

GLASSWARE: Wineglass

GARNISH: Radish wheel, dill, fennel, rosemary, olive, lemon peel

- **Barspoon kalamata olive juice**
- **3 oz. 18.21 Original Tonic**
- **3 oz. Topo Chico**
- **1½ oz. Fowler's American Style Gin**

1. Add all of the ingredients, in the order listed, to a wineglass with a single large ice cube and stir gently.
2. Be sure to slap the garnish herbs and radish to release their aromas.

CAFÉ ON COLLEGE

INDEPENDENT DISTILLING
547 EAST COLLEGE AVENUE, DECATUR

The guys at Independent Distilling love to support local brands whenever they can. This Old Fashioned interpretation uses locally made bitters.

GLASSWARE: Rocks glass

GARNISH: Candied pecan, espresso coffee beans, orange peel

- 2 oz. Independent Distilling Company Hellbender Bourbon
- Barspoon Coffee Pecan Syrup (see recipe)

- 1 pipette 18.21 Prohibition Aromatic Bitters
- Dash Fee Brothers Aztec Chocolate Bitters

1. Add all of the ingredients into a mixing glass and stir with ice.

2. Strain the cocktail over a single large ice cube into a rocks glass.

3. Garnish with candied pecan, espresso coffee beans, and orange peel.

COFFEE PECAN SYRUP: Add 1 cup Sugar in the Raw and 1 cup water into a pot and stir until the sugar is dissolved. Add 1 cup pecans, ½ cup coffee, reduce the heat, and simmer for 5 minutes. Let the syrup macerate overnight, then strain off the pecans and use them to garnish.

SOS TIKI BAR

340 CHURCH STREET, DECATUR

SOS Tiki Bar, located right around the back of the Decatur location of Victory, was started by Ian Jones and his team as an excuse "to drink a bunch of rum and fruity drinks." It is the perfect place to go when you want a totally fun, over-the-top drink that pushes the envelope on creativity, presentation, and taste. As a small bar, they easily have lines most weekend nights, and Ian estimates that they've "legitimately done hundreds and hundreds of cocktails" during SOS's existence.

For SOS Tiki Bar, Ian says, "Obviously presentation is a pretty big thing, and it can be as absurd as you have time to make it. But oftentimes, we kind of strive to find a balance thereof useful to being a little less wasteful."

One time they weren't able to fully find that balance was during the holidays. Ian describes their annual six-week Christmas menu pop-up experience as "a full-on battle," which is quite a way to describe what is supposedly the most wonderful time of the year.

One year, he remembers, "we were literally cutting up chunks of Christmas trees for decorations, so it'd be a whole branch of the tree hanging out of a drink with ornaments hanging on it, and fake coconut frosting on the top to make it look snowy. Every surface of the place was sticky and frosted with pine needles everywhere. We'd have a whole tree outside where we'd run out and snip branches off. That sort of thing was probably an example of taking presentation too far!"

LEMON PEPPER WET

Conrad Helms, named Best Bartender in 2023 by *Atlanta Magazine,* and lead bartender Christopher "Grumpy" Ford created this playful drink as a salute to Atlanta's love for lemon pepper wings. Celery is often enjoyed alongside a lemon pepper wing, which is incorporated here into the house-made celery lemon cordial. The result is tangy and refreshing, and really makes you wonder if there is any reason why a rim of lemon pepper seasoning cannot one day be as popular as Tajín is today.

GLASSWARE: Nick & Nora glass

- **Lemon pepper seasoning, for the rim**
- **1¼ oz. Caravedo Pisco Mosto Verde Acholado**
- **½ oz. Nordés Gin**
- **¼ oz. Green Chartreuse or Centum**
- **1 oz. Celery Lemon Cordial (see recipe)**
- **5 drops 20% Saline Solution (see recipe)**

1. Wet the side of Nick & Nora glass, then roll the glass in lemon pepper seasoning.

2. Combine the pisco, gin, and liqueur in a shaking tin. Then, add the cordial. Finally, add the saline solution to add saltiness.

3. Shake, then pour the cocktail into the Nick & Nora.

CELERY LEMON CORDIAL: Take 600 grams chopped celery, 200 grams water, 90 grams lemon juice, and 2 lemon peels, then blend them in a blender until smooth. Strain the mixture through cheesecloth into a bain-marie filled with ascorbic acid. Weigh the celery mixture and add 100% sugar and 12% citric acid. Whisk or blend to combine.

20% SALINE SOLUTION: Combine 8 oz. hot water with 2 oz. salt to create a 20% saline solution.

WIDOW MAKER

LAZY BETTY
1530 DEKALB AVENUE NORTHEAST

Fat-washing a spirit may seem like a strange concept, but what it does is make a drink more creamy, silky, and . . . delicious. And when you work in a Michelin-starred fine dining restaurant, *why not* use A5 Wagyu beef for your fat wash? Conrad Helms aims for a bold and weighted, apple-pie type of cocktail. The Calvados helps to accent the apple element, but also cuts through the fat with its higher proof. The Pommeau really drives home the sweet, cooked-apple flavor. Finally, the allspice bitters pulls on the notes that the rye picks up off of the barrel through its aging process, but also mimics the baking spices that appear in pie crust. Lastly, you can smoke the cocktail with cherry wood to give the experience a nice oven-roasted finish.

GLASSWARE: Rocks glass

GARNISH: Smoke, stamped ice cube

- 1½ oz. A5 Fat–Washed Rye (see recipe)
- ½ oz. Manoir de Montreuil Calvados
- ¾ oz. La Père Jules Pommeau de Normandie
- ½ oz. Spiced Syrup (see recipe)
- 3 drops Jerry Thomas bitters
- 1 drop walnut bitters

1. In a mixing glass, combine the rye, Calvados, pommeau , and syrup.
2. Then add the Jerry Thomas bitters. Stir this mixture with ice then strain it into a rocks glass.

3. Imprint a large cube with a stamp indention so as to suspend the walnut bitters. Just one drop of walnut bitters into the glass will illuminate the indention.

SPICED SYRUP: Take 1 tablespoon baking spice or pumpkin pie spice, 1 cup sugar, and 1 cup water and heat the mixture in a saucepan. Once the sugar dissolves, remove the pot from heat and let the syrup cool.

A5 FAT–WASHED RYE: Measure out 1,000 grams rye. You can make this fat-wash technique with any amount of rye, but the important part to remember when fat-washing with animal fat is to use a 20% ratio of fat to spirit, in order to solidify the fat wash (i.e., 250 grams spirit to 50 grams fat.) Take A5 fat in the form that exposes the most surface area (think ground or chopped up fine) and put it into a pot. Cover with water. Cook on low-medium heat for 30 to 45 minutes or until all of the water has cooked out, and the remaining liquid is rendered fat. There will be no more bubbles in the liquid at this state. Strain out to get just the fat, and weigh out 200 grams of this liquid. Then combine both into a bain-marie or vessel. Keep at room temperature for the next hour, stirring occasionally to mix, not emulsify, but mix the fat and the spirit together. Cover, and freeze overnight. The next day, grab it out of the freezer and take the fat cap off of the liquid. Strain the remaining liquid through cheesecloth.

THE FERRYMAN

LAZY BETTY
1530 DEKALB AVENUE NORTHEAST

Andy Han took the lead on creating this drink, The Ferryman, named after a character out of Norse mythology that is the carrier from this life to the afterlife. The Icelandic spirit in this drink, Brennivin Aquavit, is a smooth and clean spirit with subtle herbal notes. This cocktail gets a beautiful and dark hue with the mysterious purple blue color coming from a tangy plum ginger shrub. The sesame syrup brings an almost corn- or nut-like flavor, then yuzu and the shrub add some fruity and acidic notes. Umesha is a plum wine that bolsters the shrub's fruit component, and Green Chartreuse also adds an alluring aroma for a balancing touch.

GLASSWARE: Wineglass

GARNISH: Thyme sprig, flamed Chartreuse V.E.P Yellow

- 1 oz. Brennivin Aquavit
- 1 oz. umeshu
- ¾ oz. ginger liqueur
- ½ oz. Toasted Sesame Brown Sugar Syrup (see recipe)
- ½ oz. yuzu
- ½ oz. Plum Ginger Shrub (see recipe)
- Green Chartreuse, to taste

1. Add all of the ingredients into a shaking tin with ice, then double-strain the cocktail into a wineglass that contains a large square ice cube. Drop in a thyme sprig.

2. Put Chartreuse V.E.P. Yellow into a mister, ignite a butane lighter, and hold the lighter slightly above the glass, then spray the Chartreuse into the flame for a flambé effect.

TOASTED SESAME BROWN SUGAR SYRUP: Toast 200 grams black sesame seeds, stirring regularly so they don't burn. You'll know when it's ready once it starts "popping" and smoking. Add 500 grams water to deglaze the pan. Bring to a boil then simmer the seeds. Strain the seeds out and then add an equal weight of brown sugar and stir to combine.

PLUM GINGER SHRUB: Vacuum-seal 800 grams chopped plum, 20 grams chopped ginger, 400 grams white balsamic vinegar, 200 grams apple cider vinegar, and 250 grams sugar. Let the mixture sit for 24 hours, then strain.

SLEEPLESS IN SEATTLE

LAZY BETTY
1530 DEKALB AVENUE NORTHEAST

Mezcal unexpectedly forms the base of Lazy Betty's Espresso Martini. "Espresso and coffee differ majorly in flavor through the fact that espresso is predominantly smoky or roasted, and coffee has a more cooked and mellow profile. To supplement that smoky, roasted element into the cocktail that would normally be vacant with the use of coffee concentrate instead of espresso, we rely on the inherently smoky profile of mezcal to shine through," says Conrad Helms. "We infuse raw vanilla into the mezcal to soften it and assist the marriage of flavors, and what we are left with is a muted smokiness in our build." Manly Brews Cold Brew Liqueur also is green-focused and donates some of its profits toward rebuilding the Great Barrier reef, in addition to using 100% recycled glass.

GLASSWARE: Coupe glass
GARNISH: 3 espresso beans

- **3 oz. Coffee Mix (see recipe)**
- **1½ oz. Vanilla-Infused Mezcal (see recipe)**
- **½ oz. egg white**

1. Combine all of the ingredients in a cocktail shaker then reverse dry-shake—shake with ice first, then strain, then dry-shake.
2. Garnish with 3 espresso beans.

COFFEE MIX: Take 2 cups coffee concentrate, 2 cups Manly Spirits Cold Brew Coffee Liqueur, 1 cup Dows 10 Year Tawny Port, ½ cup Watershed Distillery Nocino, and ½ cup simple syrup and combine them in a large container, stirring until the ingredients are fully incorporated.

VANILLA-INFUSED MEZCAL: Vacuum-seal 1 (750 ml) bottle of Mezcal Amarás and 2 vanilla beans, sliced and opened in the middle. Leave the infusion at room temperature and agitate daily. Strain before using.

DAD'S

870 NORTH HIGHLAND AVENUE NORTHEAST

How do you create a cocktail bar in a neighborhood that's known for its taverns and dives? You create Dad's. Dad's is a plaid-filled den of a space. A space where you can get a pack of cigarettes out of a vending

machine, eat some meatloaf and disco fries, *and* enjoy an excellent Manhattan. Dad's takes maybe not a no-frills approach, but at least a low-frills approach to its cocktail menu. Unlike owner Randy Pechin's other spot, Little Spirit, there are no funkily named drinks here. Cocktails are simply named their original names, and the drinks stay relatively true to form with just minor tweaks season to season. The result is retro cool, a place you'll want to come back to time and time again.

FRENCH 75

DAD'S
870 NORTH HIGHLAND AVENUE NORTHEAST

Why not tequila up a classy French 75? Beverage director Ryan Dickey goes for a rather classic interpretation except adds equal parts gin and tequila and uses a honey simple syrup (use a 1:1 ratio, in grams weighed, of honey to water). Elderflower liqueur makes just about everything taste better, and lavender bitters add a floral finishing touch.

GLASSWARE: Coupe glass

GARNISH: Lemon twist

- ¾ oz. London dry gin
- ¾ oz. añejo tequila
- ½ oz. elderflower liqueur
- ½ oz. honey simple syrup
- ¾ oz. fresh lemon juice
- 3 dashes Scrappy's Lavender Bitters
- Lemon peel, expressed and discarded
- Prosecco, to top

1. Combine all of the ingredients, except for the prosecco, in a cocktail shaker filled with ice and shake.

2. Strain the cocktail into a coupe and top with prosecco. Garnish with a lemon twist.

APPLETINI

It's not surprising to see that the late-1990s darling, the Appletini, has a spot on the menu at a cocktail bar that's built to feel like the cozy, kitschy living room you might have grown up with. Dad's puts in the work by juicing up their apples and acid-adjusting them. Acid-adjusting is a way to adjust the acidity levels of an ingredient to achieve balance in a cocktail.

GLASSWARE: Nick & Nora glass
GARNISH: Luxardo cherry

- **1½ oz. Sobieski Vodka**

- **1½ oz. Acid-Adjusted Apple Juice (see recipe)**
- **¼ oz. simple syrup**

1. Combine all of the ingredients together in a mixing glass with ice, stir, then strain the cocktail into a Nick & Nora.

2. Garnish with a Luxardo cherry speared on a cocktail pick.

ACID-ADJUSTED APPLE JUICE: Slice 8 Granny Smith apples (toss the cores). Juice 950 grams apple slices, then strain the juice. Add 1 tablespoon citric acid and 1 tablespoon malic acid per 950 grams of apple slices juiced. Stir and blend well until the acids are fully emulsified into the juice. Bottle the juice (and be sure to label and date it).

DUBOIS DAIQUIRI

MARCUS BAR & GRILLE
525 EDGEWOOD AVENUE SOUTHEAST

Dee Sangoyele came up with this interpretation of a Daiquiri using a blend of rums. Equiano Original Rum is an additive-free African and Carribean aged rum, while Batavia-Arrack is an unaged Indonesian rum made from sugarcane and fermented red rice.

GLASSWARE: Rocks glass

GARNISH: Rosemary sprig, toasted

- 1 oz. Batavia-Arrack van Oosten
- 1 oz. Equiano Original Rum
- ¾ oz. simple syrup
- ½ oz. fresh lime juice
- ½ oz. maraschino cherry juice

1. Add all of the ingredients to a cocktail shaker with ice and shake.
2. Strain the cocktail into a rocks glass with a large ice cube.
3. Garnish with a toasted rosemary sprig.

GUNSHOW

924 GARRETT STREET

No two nights are the same at Gunshow, a Michelin-recommended restaurant headed by supremely nice human being Kevin Gillespie. Sometimes in life, you might just want a simple cheeseburger and fries, but for those nights you're wanting something a little more offbeat, a little more challenging, you go to Gunshow. There you'll find a culinary playground known for pushing the boundaries on food and drink, but in a fun and casual atmosphere. Chefs come around table to table—not unlike the interactive style of food service you receive at dim sum restaurants—and present the dishes they've created. Cocktails are also presented tableside, like the crowd-pleasing Toasted Old Fashioned, which is a show and drink all in one. While that cocktail is always on the menu, the menu is otherwise ever-changing. "The concept is that there is no concept," says beverage director Jeramie Eubanks. "It's a blank slate; we're not tied to doing Southern food, Indian food, Mediterranean food. It's just, do whatever you want to do."

TOASTED OLD FASHIONED

GUNSHOW
924 GARRETT STREET

I've had the Toasted Old Fashioned a number of times now at Gunshow, but it never fails to draw out a totally involuntary, "Oh, wowww!" even though I know what's coming. It's extraordinarily tasty, simply a great and simple Old Fashioned. Gunshow shares step-by-step instructions for how to recreate it at home. Put the work in to show off on date night or at a dinner party to truly impress your guests.

GLASSWARE: Rocks glass

- 2 oz. bourbon
- ¼ oz. Burnt Sugar Syrup (see recipe)
- 3 controlled top dashes of Fee Brothers Old Fashioned Aromatic Bitters
- 4 controlled top dashes of Orange Bitters Blend (see recipe)
- Sugared Cinnamon Stick (see recipe)
- 151 demerara rum, to flame
- Orange peel

1. Add the bourbon, syrup, and bitters to a rocks glass.

2. Add ice and stir until a slight sheen is seen outside of the glass.

3. Place the cinnamon stick across one edge of the glass, drizzle with 151 demerara rum (Hamilton or Lemon Hart work great!), and light the stick on fire. Express an orange peel over the flame and let the stick cook until the sugars bubble.

4. Blow out the flame and nudge the cinnamon stick into the glass using the orange peel. Wipe orange oils on the rim of the glass and place the peel perpendicularly over the cinnamon stick, creating an X to guide the drinker toward the cool side.

BURNT SUGAR SYRUP: Place 8 cups sugar in a pot over medium-high heat on an induction burner. Cook down to a dark liquid consistency. Remove the pot from heat and let the sugar cool for 10 minutes. Slowly add 4 cups water (BE CAREFUL!) and stir until well incorporated. Add the pot back to heat and cook until well integrated and rich. Let cool.

ORANGE BITTERS BLEND: Blend 2 (5 oz.) bottles Fee Brothers West Indian Orange Bitters with 1 (5 oz.) bottle Regans' Orange Bitters No. 6.

SUGARED CINNAMON STICK: Add cinnamon sticks to a bowl and lightly coat them with bourbon, as needed. Layer a cookie sheet with sugar, as needed, and place the damp cinnamon sticks on top, gently burying them a little. Cover with another layer of sugar and let them sit overnight in a cool, dry place.

ATL STREET SOUR

GUNSHOW
924 GARRETT STREET

This drink created by beverage director Jeramie Eubanks is a lemon pepper wing in liquid form—literally. It's extraordinarily popular; Gunshow's diners love it! Jeramie uses chickens from local farmers to create the fat-washed gin.

GLASSWARE: Collins glass

GARNISH: Lemon twist, expressed

- 2 oz. Chicken Fat & Thyme Gin (see recipe)
- ¾ oz. 6% Citric Acid Solution (see recipe)
- ¾ oz. Honey Lemon-Pepper Syrup (see recipe)
- 1 gram 25% Saline Solution (see recipe on page 195)

1. Shake all of the ingredients together in a cocktail shaker, then double-strain the cocktail over a large chunk of ice into a collins glass.

2. Express a lemon twist over the drink, then add the twist as a garnish. Cut it all pretty because this is Atlanta, after all!

CHICKEN FAT & THYME GIN: Melt 5 oz. chicken fat. Pour the fat into a 2-quart mason jar along with 1 (750 ml) bottle of Murrell's Row Tulsi Gin and 20 grams fresh thyme. Tighten the jar lid and stick the jar in a sous vide circulator bath at 155°F (68°C) for 2 hours. Take the jar out of the bath and allow it to come to room temperature. Then, transfer the jar to the freezer and let it freeze overnight, or 12 hours. Strain the gin through a fine-mesh strainer and then again through a coffee filter. Store in the refrigerator for up to 1 month.

6% CITRIC ACID SOLUTION: Weigh 6 grams citric acid powder and 100 grams hot water and whisk together until the citric acid powder has dissolved into the water. Store in the refrigerator for up to 1 month.

HONEY LEMON-PEPPER SYRUP: Take 32 oz. honey, 16 oz. water, and 4 tablespoons lemon pepper seasoning and cook in a pot, constantly stirring until it boils. Let the syrup steep for 2 hours and then strain it through a fine-mesh strainer. Refrigerate for up to 1 month.

SUMMER TONIC

GUNSHOW
924 GARRETT STREET

Gunshow works with over thirty local farmers, and when it's summer squash season, they love to nab some fresh squash and use it in their food and cocktails. Jeramie Eubanks toiled with the ratios in this drink until he was able to pull through both the squash and curry flavors. You get the sweetness from the yellow squash and a hit of acidity from the citric acid solution, and the end result is a flavorful and well-balanced drink that, yes, tastes like a delicious curry!

GLASSWARE: Collins or double rocks glass

GARNISH: Pineapple sage

- 2 oz. Curry-Infused Vodka (see recipe)
- 1 oz. Squash Syrup (see recipe)
- ¼ oz. 25% Citric Acid Solution (see recipe)
- 1 gram 25% Saline Solution (see recipe)
- Fever-Tree Mediterranean Tonic Water, to top

1. Add all of the ingredients, except the tonic water, into a collins or double rocks glass and add ice.

2. Stir to incorporate for 5 seconds, then top with the tonic water. Gently dip your barspoon into the glass to incorporate the tonic water.

3. Have fun with the garnish. Gunshow's partner farmers were bringing in gorgeous and aromatic pineapple sage during the summer, so they used that!

CURRY-INFUSED VODKA: Take 3 tablespoons Madras curry and 1 liter vodka and let them sit together in a covered container overnight. Strain the vodka through a coffee filter–lined fine-mesh strainer and bottle. Refrigerate for up to 1 month.

SQUASH SYRUP: Juice yellow summer squash (any squash will work but will also change the flavor profile quite a bit, so experiment!). Run your squash juice through a coffee filter–lined fine-mesh strainer and then weigh your juice. Add your juice to a pot with equal parts by weight sugar. Cook until the sugar is dissolved and fully incorporated into the squash juice. Store in the refrigerator for up to 1 week.

25% CITRIC ACID SOLUTION: Weigh 250 grams citric acid powder and 1,000 grams hot water and whisk until the citric acid powder has dissolved into the water. Store in the refrigerator for up to 1 month.

25% SALINE SOLUTION: Whisk together 4 oz. kosher salt and 16 oz. hot water until the salt is dissolved into the water. Store in the refrigerator for up to 1 month.

ELA

1186 NORTH HIGHLAND AVENUE NORTHEAST

Ela proves that an old dog can learn new tricks. Ela is the newest creation from the team behind South City Kitchen, which has been a stalwart in the Atlanta dining scene since 1993. Ela is a pan-Mediterranean restaurant where you can expect to enjoy big, bold spices amidst entrees of fresh seafood and lamb. Their bar program, created by beverage director Ian Mendelsohn, matches these daring, punchy flavors.

CRETAN BULL

Beverage director Ian Mendelsohn had a fantastic time exploring the spices and the flavors endemic to the Middle East region when developing the drink menu for Ela. Baharat, a staple Middle Eastern spice blend incorporating cardamom, cumin, cloves, nutmeg, and more, forms a rich base to this Manhattan riff. Verino's Tentura Antica adds even more cinnamon flavor.

GLASSWARE: Coupe glass

GARNISH: Luxardo cherry

- 1 oz. American Spirit Works Fiddler Unison Bourbon
- 1 oz. American Spirit Works Resurgens Rye
- ½ oz. Verino Tentura Antica Cinnamon Liqueur
- ¼ oz. Fernet-Branca
- ¼ oz. Baharat Rich Syrup (see recipe)
- 2 dashes aromatic bitters

1. Chill a coupe glass. Add all of the ingredients to a mixing glass. Add ice and stir for 15 seconds.
2. Strain the cocktail into the chilled coupe. Garnish with a Luxardo cherry speared on a cocktail pick.

BAHARAT RICH SYRUP: Add 16 oz. demerara sugar, 8 oz. hot water, and 1 tablespoon Baharat (see recipe) spice blend into a pot. Bring the mixture to a simmer until the sugar is dissolved. Remove the syrup from heat and let sit for 1 hour. Strain it through a chinois.

BAHARAT: Add 1 tablespoon ground black pepper, 1 teaspoon ground cloves, 2 teaspoons ground nutmeg, 1 teaspoon ground cumin, 2 teaspoons paprika, 1 teaspoon kosher salt, 1 teaspoon ground coriander, ¼ teaspoon ground cardamom, and 1 teaspoon ground cinnamon to a container and stir to combine.

ROYAL GROVE

Middle Eastern countries like Iran and Turkey are some of the world's biggest grape producers, so beverage director Ian Mendelsohn sought to pay homage by crafting a cocktail that highlights some of the region's most beautiful produce. The end result is a refreshing, sweet, and fun way to get your fruits in for the day. Use a 2 oz. mister for the garnish.

GLASSWARE: Nick & Nora glass

GARNISH: Absinthe mist

- 1½ oz. Stray Dog Wild Gin
- ¾ oz. Grape Syrup (see recipe)
- ¾ oz. fresh lemon juice
- ½ oz. Amaro Montenegro
- 2 dashes orange bitters
- 3 dashes Fee Brothers Fee Foam

1. Add all of the ingredients to a cocktail shaker. Dry-shake hard and then add ice.

2. Shake again. Double-strain the cocktail into a Nick & Nora. Garnish with absinthe mist.

GRAPE SYRUP: Wash and destem 24 oz. red table grapes. Add them to a saucepan with 2 oz. granulated sugar and heat until the sugar is dissolved. Press the grapes until they burst and release their juices. Remove the pot from heat and pass the mixture through a food mill to discard the seeds and stems. Strain the remaining juice through a fine-mesh strainer and place the juice back into the pot. Turn on the heat and hard-simmer the syrup until the volume is reduced by 30%. Let the syrup cool.

3 STACKS

Tequila and pineapple juice are a match made in heaven, but cold brew? Don't knock it until you try it, because these flavors combine to make for a delicious blend. This drink is a cult favorite, and a go-to drink its creator Timothy Parker likes to make for parties. Find this drink at the impossibly cool SoCal-inspired taco and burrito spot Muchacho. For the orgeat, Muchacho's team recommends BG Reynolds, though you can ultimately use your personal favorite. 3 Stacks is named in reference to Parker's favorite hip-hop artist of all time, Andre 3000.

GLASSWARE: Rocks glass

GARNISH: Lime wheel, pineapple fronds, grated nutmeg

- 2 oz. blanco tequila
- 1 oz. pineapple juice
- ½ oz. fresh lime juice
- ½ oz. BG Reynolds Original Orgeat Cocktail Syrup
- ¼ oz. cold brew coffee

1. Combine all of the ingredients in a cocktail shaker with ice and shake hard.

2. Strain the cocktail into a rocks glass filled with ice cubes.

3. Garnish with a lime wheel, pineapple fronds, and nutmeg.

GRANT PARK SOCIAL

790 GLENWOOD AVENUE SOUTHEAST SUITE 250

Step through a discreet black door, and that's where you'll discover Grant Park Social—a small but mighty whiskey bar serving up a selection of 250 varieties of whiskeys. While bourbon takes center stage, Grant Park Social also boasts a selection of scotches, Japanese whiskeys, and other spirits. Grant Park Social is a quaint place, with just twelve seats at the bar. Customers sometimes say it feels like their dream basement.

Manned by the gregarious Colton Harris, this bar is certainly in good hands. "There's a sexy, grown vibe to it, but you're not going to feel out of place here in a T-shirt and a baseball cap. It's all kinds of people that drink whiskey, not just rich old guys. We have it set up so you're not distracted by the TV. I want you to have conversations with people," Colton says.

He likes to take time to hunt on the secondary market for good whiskeys and special releases, so that "we're able to offer you something you may not have the chance to taste otherwise."

But what excites him most these days about the world of whiskey is that women are now getting involved. "Whiskey has for such a long time been one way. We're now reaching a point where it's diversifying. There are a lot more women that are getting involved in making whiskey. There's George Dickel, their master distiller is female; Woodford Reserve, female; of course Uncle Nearest, female master distiller. I'm really digging that it's bringing some different flavor profiles to whiskey," says Colton. "Women are coming to the game and changing the way we experience whiskey. The newfound female presence in the whiskey world, and just culturally too, more cultures are getting involved in making whiskey, that's the most exciting thing I can think of for something that's been around for such a long time."

HONEY HIBISCUS PALOMA

GRANT PARK SOCIAL
790 GLENWOOD AVENUE SOUTHEAST SUITE 250

Grant Park Social adds a frothy egg white top to a classic Paloma and serves it up in a coupe glass. Garnish it with some dried hibiscus flowers and a dehydrated lemon wheel. A Paloma has never looked sexier!

GLASSWARE: Coupe glass

GARNISH: Hibiscus flowers, dehydrated lemon wheel

- 2 oz. reposado tequila
- 2 oz. grapefruit juice
- ¾ oz. fresh lime juice
- ¾ oz. egg white
- ½ oz. agave nectar

1. Add all of the ingredients to a shaker and dry-shake to combine.
2. Add ice and wet-shake, then strain the cocktail into a coupe and garnish with hibiscus flowers and a dehydrated lemon wheel.

RED MOON OVER MANHATTAN

GRANT PARK SOCIAL
790 GLENWOOD AVENUE SOUTHEAST SUITE 250

The Manhattan gets a twist with this Red Moon Over Manhattan, which is still spirit-forward but also tastes a bit like mulled wine. Use bourbon or rye for the spirit.

GLASSWARE: Rocks glass
GARNISH: 3 Luxardo cherries

- 2 oz. red wine
- 1 oz. bourbon
- ½ oz. simple syrup

1. Stir all of the ingredients to combine in a mixing glass.
2. Pour the cocktail into a rocks glass over one large square ice cube.
3. Garnish with 3 Luxardo cherries on a cocktail pick.

WARM WINTER

GRANT PARK SOCIAL
790 GLENWOOD AVENUE SOUTHEAST SUITE 250

Bourbon is a favorite for Grant Park Social's beverage director, Colton Harris, so it makes sense that even in a tequila drink, he adds a little bit of bourbon. It makes for a boozy match made in heaven, and the bitters and cinnamon stick add a finishing touch.

GLASSWARE: Rocks glass

GARNISH: Orange twist; cinnamon stick, smoked

- 1½ oz. reposado tequila
- ½ oz. bourbon
- ¼ oz. orange juice
- ¼ oz. simple syrup
- 3 dashes Angostura bitters
- 2 dashes orange bitters

1. Add all of the ingredients into a mixing glass, then stir to combine.
2. Pour the cocktail into a rocks glass over one large ice cube.
3. Garnish with an orange twist and cinnamon stick, smoking the end of the stick for the perfect smoky finish.

VESPER

924 GARRETT STREET SUITE D

Vesper co-owner Damien McGee's late father had a lot of love for James Bond. To pay tribute, he created Vesper, an elegant lounge that he hopes is somewhere "James Bond might hang out at when he wasn't killing people." The result is a moody, cozy cocktail lounge—with great nonalcoholic offerings as well—that's quickly building a group of regulars who can always come to Vesper for a great Martini.

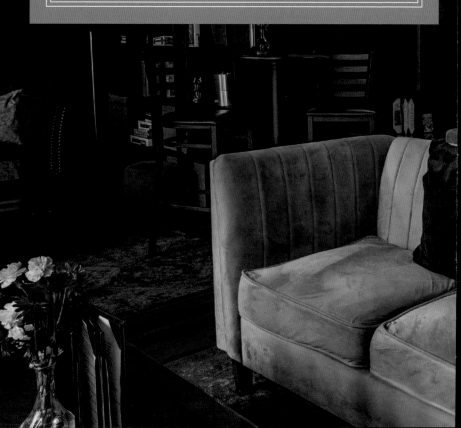

THE VESPER

VESPER
924 GARRETT STREET SUITE D

Vesper's alluring namesake drink feels like something you'd like to enjoy while sitting elegantly outside of a French café. Garnish with an orange twist rather than a lemon twist for a bit of fun. To get an ice-cold glass at home, Damien McGee says you can simply fill your martini glass with ice and cold water, let it sit for 10 minutes, and it'll be perfectly chilled.

GLASSWARE: Martini glass

GARNISH: Orange twist

- 2 oz. Ketel One Vodka
- 1 oz. St. George Terroir Gin
- ¾ oz. Cocchi Americano

1. Chill a martini glass. Combine all of the ingredients in a mixing glass, stir, then serve in the chilled martini glass.

2. Garnish with an orange twist.

DAMIEN'S MANHATTAN

VESPER
924 GARRETT STREET SUITE D

Damien's Manhattan is a little richer, a little darker than a standard Manhattan. Serve it up nice and cold in a chilled martini glass (see page 214). Damien McGee says it tastes like Christmas because of the vermouth and the bitters. Then of course, Luxardo cherries go well with just about everything.

GLASSWARE: Martini glass

GARNISH: Luxardo cherry

- **2 oz. Angel's Envy Kentucky Straight Bourbon**
- **¾ oz. BROVO Jammy Sweet Vermouth**
- **¾ oz. Luxardo Cherries syrup, from the can or jar**
- **3 shakes 18.21 Bitters Prohibition Aromatic Bitters**

1. Chill a martini glass. Combine all of the ingredients in a mixing glass, stir, then serve in the chilled martini glass.
2. Garnish with a Luxardo cherry speared on a cocktail pick.

KATIE MCDONALD, BANSHEE

In a neighborhood much more known for loving a PBR and a shot of Jameson, Banshee is a funky, cool standout, with great food and craft cocktails, still fitting right into East Atlanta's eclectic scene. It's seasonal, delicious upscale food in a relaxed atmosphere. At night, there's a vibe shift with great music, dancing, and even hot dogs for a late-night nosh. For all the team's hard work, Banshee recently won a Bib Gourmand distinction from the Michelin guide, which is the guide's award for great food at great values.

Banshee is a dream come true in that it was started by a group of friends and industry veterans—Peter Chvala, Nolan Wynn, Katie McDonald, and Faielle Bolzan Stocco—who had all talked over the years about having a place to call their own one day.

"We were all working hard for really good people, but we wanted to work hard for ourselves," says Katie McDonald, the beverage director.

Katie first cut her teeth as a bartender under Paul Calvert at Sound Table, a popular but now-shuttered bar in Atlanta's hot spot for night-life, Edgewood. Later, she learned all about beer at Wrecking Bar before eventually teaming up with her partners to start Banshee.

One thing that sets Banshee's drinks menu apart is the use of homemade shrubs. "I love to make shrubs," says Katie. "[A shrub is] a fruit-and-vinegar-based syrup. It's a beautiful combination of sweet, sour, and fruit. Shrubs offer a lot of different things to find that balance in a cocktail."

Another thing that excites McDonald in the cocktail world is the growing popularity of tequila and mezcal. "More specifically, smaller, family-owned productions," she says. "It doesn't have to be celebrity-endorsed or a big brand name that you've heard in all the songs, people really are trying to find those smaller brands and the family-owned brands. We like to support small businesses, support local, and people are doing that with their spirits as well."

STATELY HAG

BANSHEE
1271 GLENWOOD AVENUE SOUTHEAST

This drink has been on the menu at Banshee since its beginnings in 2018. Strega, an Italian aperitivo, balances the Cocchi Americano to create this bright and herbaceous tequila-based drink. Partner and beverage director Katie McDonald makes sure that everyone who works at the bar tastes any cocktail she puts on the menu to ensure each drink has the perfect balance.

GLASSWARE: Coupe glass

GARNISH: Lemon twist, expressed; thyme, expressed

- ¾ oz. reposado tequila
- ¾ oz. Liquore Strega
- ¾ oz. Cocchi Americano
- ¾ oz. fresh lemon juice

1. Chill a coupe glass. Combine all of the ingredients in a cocktail shaker with ice and shake.

2. Double-strain the cocktail into the chilled coupe.

3. Express a lemon twist and thyme over the drink, then add both as garnishes.

CARELESS WHISPER #2

BANSHEE
1271 GLENWOOD AVENUE SOUTHEAST

Banshee's beverage director, Katie McDonald, uses a house-made Strawberry-Tarragon Shrub to add depth, complexity, and a tangy kick to Careless Whisper #2. Cahaça, a fermented sugarcane juice, forms the base of this drink. Forthave Red Aperitivo is an American-made aperitivo that adds even more herbal notes.

GLASSWARE: Collins glass

GARNISH: Tarragon sprig

- 1 oz. Novo Fogo Silver Cachaça
- 1 oz. Strawberry-Tarragon Shrub (see recipe)
- ½ oz. Forthave Red Aperitivo
- Barspoon fresh lime juice
- Cava, to top

1. Combine all of the ingredients, except for the cava, in a cocktail shaker with ice and give it a quick hard shake.

2. Double-strain the cocktail into a collins glass filled 80% with ice.

3. Top with cava.

4. Stir to combine and garnish with a tarragon sprig.

Strawberry-Tarragon Shrub: A shrub is generally equal parts fruit, sugar, and vinegar. Dice strawberries, as needed. Combine with white sugar, massaging the granules into the fruit. Tear tarragon, to taste, add it to the mixture, and work it in thoroughly. (For every 8 pounds of strawberries, McDonald uses about ½ pound of tarragon.) Cover tightly and keep in a cool, dark area for at least 1 day to macerate. The sugar will pull the juice out of the fruit. After a day or so, massage the fruit to release any residual juices. Leave the fruit in. Add apple cider vinegar, to taste, and stir to combine. Cover the shrub again and allow it to sit 1 more day in the same cool, dark place. Almost done! Open the container and squeeze the fruit again. Then, strain out the berries and tarragon, taking time to press all the liquid out of the pulp. Finally, add more apple cider vinegar (a little bit at a time; you can always add more but can't take it away!) to reach the desired tartness.

LEXINGTON LAYOVER

BANSHEE
1271 GLENWOOD AVENUE SOUTHEAST

This isn't your average bourbon drink. The Lexington Layover incorporates tropical flavors like pineapple juice and orgeat for a tiki take that totally works.

GLASSWARE: Rocks glass

GARNISH: Angostura mist

- 1½ oz. bourbon
- ½ oz. Mattei Cap Corse Blanc Quinquina
- ¼ oz. Heering Cherry Liqueur
- ¼ oz. fresh lime juice
- ¼ oz. pineapple juice
- Barspoon Easy Orgeat (see recipe)

1. Combine all of the ingredients in a cocktail shaker with ice and shake.

2. Double-strain the cocktail into a chilled rocks glass over fresh ice. Garnish with Angostura mist (7 to 8 sprays of Angostura in an atomizer).

EASY ORGEAT: Combine 2 cups almond milk and 4 cups sugar in a saucepan and heat until all of the sugar is dissolved. Remove from heat and add 2 tablespoons almond extract, ⅓ cup cognac or brandy, and 1 tablespoon orange flower water. Stir to combine.

BLACKEST HEART

BANSHEE
1271 GLENWOOD AVENUE SOUTHEAST

Rye whiskey gets the Italian treatment with a mix of Italian diges-
tifs. The result is a stiff, bitter drink fit for the blackest of hearts.

GLASSWARE: Rocks glass

GARNISH: Lemon twist, expressed

- ¾ oz. rye
- ¾ oz. Cynar
- ¾ oz. Amaro Averna

- Half-barspoon Caffè Borghetti

1. Chill a rocks glass. Combine all of the ingredients in a mixing glass and stir.
2. Serve the cocktail in the chilled rocks glass over a large cube.
3. Express a lemon twist over the cocktail, then add the twist as a garnish.

A LEAVE OF ABSINTHE

LEON'S FULL SERVICE
131 EAST PONCE DE LEON AVENUE, DECATUR

Have you ever tried absinthe? This cocktail at LEON's featuring the French aperitif gets juuust a touch of it to add some bitterness. Tonic water adds effervescence, and lemon juice rounds it out with some acidity.

GLASSWARE: Collins glass

GARNISH: Orange peel, expressed

- 1 teaspoon St. George Absinthe
- ½ oz. fresh lemon juice
- 1½ oz. Kina l'Aero d'Or
- Fever-Tree Tonic Water, to top

1. Build the cocktail, in the order of ingredients listed, except for the tonic water, in a collins glass with ice.

2. Top with Fever-Tree Tonic Water.

3. Stir to combine. Express an orange peel over the drink, then add the peel as a garnish.

LA BEFANA

LEON'S FULL SERVICE
131 EAST PONCE DE LEON AVENUE, DECATUR

La Befana is a longtime staple on the cocktail menu at LEON's. Cocchi Storico Vermouth di Torino brings in some earthy flavors, and the Italian herbal liqueur Liquore Strega brings in a medley of botanical notes. Herbsaint is a go-to in sidecars, and fits well here in this spirit-forward drink.

GLASSWARE: Coupe or Nick & Nora glass

GARNISH: Grapefruit peel, expressed; Herbsaint spritzes

- 1 oz. 100 proof rye whiskey
- ½ oz. Cocchi Storico Vermouth di Torino
- ½ oz. Liquore Strega
- ½ oz. Cioco Liquore di Carciofo (or Cynar)
- ½ oz. Luxardo Bitter Bianco
- 2 dashes Hella Eucalyptus Bitters

1. Stir all of the ingredients together in a frozen glass to chill and serve the cocktail in a small coupe or Nick & Nora, rinsed with 2 atomized spritzes of Herbsaint.

2. Express a grapefruit peel over the drink, then add the peel as a garnish.

DR. NEMESIS

LEON'S FULL SERVICE
131 EAST PONCE DE LEON AVENUE, DECATUR

Apple Brandy is the shining star in this drink full of fall flavors. LEON's recommends ASW Armour & Oak or Watershed Apple Brandy, but you can ultimately use your favorite.

GLASSWARE: Rocks glass

GARNISH: Lightly torched star anise

- **2 oz. apple brandy**
- **¾ oz. fresh lemon juice**
- **½ oz. Honey Syrup (see recipe)**
- **½ oz. Ginger Syrup (see recipe)**
- **2 dashes Bitter Truth Decanter Bitters**
- **2 dashes Scrappy's Cardamom Bitters**

1. Shake all of the ingredients and served in a rocks glass with a single large ice cube.

2. Lightly torch a star anise and add it as a garnish.

HONEY SYRUP: In a container, combine 3 parts honey to 1 part warm, filtered water and mix well.

GINGER SYRUP: In a saucepan, combine 1 cup water and 2 cups sugar and bring to a simmer. Add 1 cup fresh ginger, finely chopped, or ginger juice. Stir until the sugar is dissolved and let the syrup cool and steep. Strain.

NEGRONI

NO. 246
129 EAST PONCE DE LEON AVENUE, DECATUR

No. 246 is a red-sauce, classic Italian restaurant in Decatur that serves up a great half-size portion of a Negroni they call The Tiny Negroni, which is super chilled in a mini martini glass. The recipe below is for a full-size portion.

GLASSWARE: Rocks glass

GARNISH: Orange coin (punch a round shape out of peeled citrus), expressed

- 1¼ oz. Bordiga Occitan Gin
- ¾ oz. Bristow Gin
- ¾ oz. Campari
- ½ oz. Punt e Mes
- ½ oz. Cocchi Storico Vermouth di Torino
- ¼ oz. St. George Bruto Americano

1. Chill a rocks glass. Combine all of the ingredients in a mixing glass and stir.

2. Chill the cocktail in an airtight bottle in your freezer, then pour it into the chilled rocks glass.

3. Express an orange coin over the drink, then add it as garnish.

OUR CITY'S CRAFT BREWERIES

Fancy yourself a brew rather than some bourbon? Craft beer is huge in Atlanta, and there's an excellent IPA on nearly every corner of Atlanta now. Here are some of the local favorites.

SWEETWATER COMPANY
195 OTTLEY DRIVE NORTHEAST

The OG in Atlanta for craft brews. IPAs are their specialty, but they have lagers, ales, and even seltzers if you're looking for something a little lighter. Try the 420 IPA for an Atlanta classic.

HIPPIN HOPS BREWERY
1308 GLENWOOD AVENUE SOUTHEAST

Hippin Hops is the state's first African American–owned brewery. Enjoy your hops alongside some hip-hop! The kitchen also whips up some delicious oysters and fried seafood; why settle for your basic burger when you can enjoy Cajun crawfish egg rolls instead?

ARCHES BREWING
3361 DOGWOOD DRIVE, HAPEVILLE

Arches creates refreshing ales and lagers in Hapeville, near Atlanta's airport. Think easy, drinkable beers that pair well with food. Their patio is also a great hang in the summertime.

ATLANTA'S BELTLINE

EVEREADY	BIJOU
TICONDEROGA CLUB	ESPRESSO MARTINI
ESPRESSO EN NOIR	SOUTHSIDE
LOST IN TRANSLATION	EL CAPITAN
MARTA EXPRESS	TRUTH AND CONSEQUENCES
MO LYCHEE	LIFE OF LEISURE
KOKOMO	LAID BACK
SOUTHERN SMOKE	
FIGGIE SMALLS	PINEAPPLE PURPLE SKY
SNAP, CRACKLE, WAP	SAUDI MONEY
GROW A PEAR	DUBAI DRIFT
THREE DOTS & A DASH	

The BeltLine is an adaptive reuse project that repurposes old railroad lines into paved pathways that will soon encompass all of Atlanta. The BeltLine not only offers a scenic journey through the city, but it also serves as a canvas for public artwork. No other recent project or development has had a bigger impact on this city's fabric, shaping its identity in both positive and challenging ways.

On any given Saturday afternoon, thousands of Atlantans will bike, stroll, and even rollerblade along the BeltLine, hopping from restaurants to cocktail bars to breweries. Dig into some of the best restaurant beverage programs and bars that are just a stone's throw away from Atlanta's BeltLine.

Local fun fact: Upwards of 2 million people visit the Atlanta BeltLine yearly.

TICONDEROGA CLUB

99 KROG STREET NORTHEAST

In a city that's becoming increasingly inundated with restaurants that are obvious cash grabs, having a genuine treasure like the Ticonderoga Club, clearly built around a passion for food and drink, is a rare delight.

Ticonderoga Club opened in 2015 as a joint venture by seasoned Atlanta food and beverage industry professionals Greg Best, David Bies, Paul Calvert, Bart Sasso and Regan Smith. It's a come-as-you-are type of place, named after a fort in New York. Walk inside the Ticonderoga Club, located in the back corner of bustling Krog Street Market, and it certainly feels like you're in the hull of a cozy, wooden ship.

If you step inside on any given evening, you'll find an eclectic mix of customers. Neighborhood regulars come for a bite and a drink to unwind after work. Groups of friends will order the Chuck Wagon, a 48 oz. chuck roast that is great for communal meals. You'll certainly find epicureans who flock to Ticonderoga Club because of its critical acclaim. And always, you'll find people ponied up at the bar, eager to savor some of Atlanta's finest handcrafted cocktails.

The truth is you simply can't talk about the craft cocktail scene in Atlanta today without talking about Ticonderoga Club. Ask any bartender in Atlanta where they look for inspiration, and nine times out of ten they're going to say it's what Greg Best and Paul Calvert are doing at Ticonderoga Club. It's a place that has such hype that, if you're anything like me and until recently, you've never been and keep hearing about it, you kind of start to wonder, okay, what exactly is going on here? Is a fire-breathing dragon going to serve me my drink, or what?

The answer I discovered is something much simpler than that. It's a lot of studying, understanding the history of drinks, and knowing what it means to make a "classic" cocktail. It's learning how to make a classic through a modern lens, while still respecting where it came from. It's taking lessons from your travels and time spent living in other cities.

Take, for example, their signature drink, the Ticonderoga Cup. The Club's ship-like atmosphere sometimes gets them mistaken for a tiki lounge, but this rum punch is not a tiki drink, but actually their way of paying homage to history, since rum punch was the drink of choice in the colonial United States.

Then, consider the Eveready, a mezcal cocktail made with ginger, lime, and cassis. Mezcal cocktails in Atlanta can sometimes fall short on balance, leading me to generally steer clear of the spirit altogether. Yet, with just one taste of this drink, I became a mezcal convert. It's just the right amount of sweet, and of course, smoky, but not overwhelmingly so.

"An overarching theme for our cocktails is that we strive for something you can continue to make years from now," says Alec Bales, lead bartender. "I was looking at some old menus, to take one of the current drinks away and put an old one back on, and what was really exciting to see is that there aren't a lot of things we can't still make."

So great, simple cocktails that you can make for years and years to come? You start to get a sense from Ticonderoga Club that maybe it's history they're trying to make. They're certainly well on their way.

EVEREADY

TICONDEROGA CLUB
99 KROG STREET NORTHEAST

The Eveready is a balanced approach to mezcal that incorporates a house-made ginger syrup and gets much of its flavor and its color from cassis liqueur, a sweet, dark-red liqueur made from black currant.

GLASSWARE: Rocks glass

GARNISH: Cucumber slice

- 1½ oz. mezcal
- ¾ oz. fresh lime juice
- ½ oz. Ginger Syrup (see recipe)
- ½ oz. cassis liqueur

1. Shake all of the ingredients in a cocktail shaker with ice.

2. Double-strain the cocktail into a rocks glass with one ice cube.

3. Garnish with a cucumber slice

GINGER SYRUP: Using a bar scale, weigh out approximately 4 pounds raw ginger: 4 pounds raw ginger will yield approximately 1,000 grams of liquid ginger juice. Wash the ginger in warm water. Using a spoon, roughly peel the skin from the ginger root. Do not be precious about this: remove most of the skin, but don't waste time trying to get it all. Once the root is skinned, roughly chop the ginger. Process the chopped ginger in the blender, adding about 2 cups hot water for every full blender pitcher. Once the ginger is completely blended into a wet pulp, strain it through a sieve. Using a ladle, press all of the juice from the ginger pulp and set the juice aside. Discard the pulp. Weigh the juice using a scale. Transfer the juice to a saucepan. Weigh out an equal part of raw cane sugar and combine it with the juice in the saucepan. Set it over medium heat and stir until well combined. Do not boil. Bottle the syrup, date it, and refrigerate for up to 2 weeks.

TICONDEROGA CLUB

TICONDEROGA CLUB
99 KROG STREET NORTHEAST

This homage to colonial Rum Punch is served in a cup that's pretty much entirely unique to Ticonderoga Club. It's a bulbous, somewhat tiki-inspired, hammered copper cup that is—dare I say it—a little ugly? Nevertheless, this kitschy cup and the tasty drink that goes inside it have become emblematic of Ticonderoga Club.

GLASSWARE: Ticonderoga Cup

GARNISH: Mint sprig

- 1½ oz. aged rum
- 1 oz. cognac
- ½ oz. fresh lemon juice
- ½ oz. Pineapple Cordial (see recipe)
- ½ oz. cream sherry

1. Shake all of the ingredients together in a cocktail shaker with ice.
2. Strain the cocktail into a Ticonderoga Cup over crushed ice, break up the ice, then top with more crushed ice. Garnish with a mint sprig and serve with a straw.

PINEAPPLE CORDIAL: Peel and core 4 ripe, golden pineapples, cutting the fruit into spears off the core. Using an electric juicer, juice the pineapple spears. Weigh the pineapple juice. Add it to a large saucepan. Weigh out half the amount each of cane sugar, white sugar, and water. For example, if the pineapple juice weighs 1,200 grams, weigh out 600 grams cane sugar, 600 grams white sugar, and 600 grams water. Add the mixture to the saucepan and mix well with a whisk. Place the saucepan over high heat until the mixture begins to boil. Once boiling, turn the heat down to medium-low so that the mixture simmers. Set a timer for 45 minutes, being sure to check on the mixture every 10 minutes or so to make sure it isn't bubbling over. Whisk well when you check on it. Once the mixture has been simmering for at least 45 minutes and it has reduced in volume by about 20%, remove it from heat. The cordial should be a rich, golden color. Allow it to cool. It will last 3 weeks in the refrigerator.

THE JAMES ROOM

661 AUBURN AVENUE NORTHEAST SUITE 280

While walking on Atlanta's BeltLine, you may come across a simple Parisian café where you can enjoy fine pastries and cappuccinos in the daytime. But if you walk inside and slip through one of its doors, you'll find one of Atlanta's swankiest, sexiest lounges: the James Room. Think speakeasy, with luxurious leather couches and glamorous touches throughout.

After a long career in nightlife, Harold Brinkley, who owns the James Room alongside his business partner, Justin Miller, took over the cocktail bar from its previous owner because he wanted to be a part of something a little more grown and sexy. He says the James Room is "intended to be unassuming. It's intended to feel like it's a place that shouldn't be doing what it's doing. It's a juxtaposition between visual presentation and sound."

The music at the James Room is a point of pride for Brinkley. He notes, without judgment of the restaurants in question, that a lot of restaurants in Atlanta will shy away from playing hip-hop and reggaeton out of a fear of creating a too-rowdy atmosphere. However, he says the James Room has found a way to incorporate and celebrate these styles of music while still having an elevated and sophisticated atmosphere: "One of our biggest compliments is, 'We love you all's music.' It's not just hip-hop music; it's R&B, it's pop, it's all things relevant to music, what's current, what's trending, but all done in a tasteful manner."

Had he not had the opportunity to buy the James Room, Brinkley says, "I don't think I would have gotten approved to be in that space as an African American operator. Sometimes our barriers to entry are a lot higher when it comes to participating in Class A real estate projects. We're overvetted and not oftentimes presented the same opportunity to be somewhere like the Buckhead shops or Ponce City Market or the Interlock."

While Brinkley acknowledges that there are African American owners in those spaces, they are few and far between, "particularly when it comes to anything with music and alcohol. The first thing [lenders] start talking about is, 'It's not going to be a nightclub, right? There's not going to be any hookah?'"

To complement the James Room's sophisticated atmosphere, Brinkley says his "goal is to get two-ingredient drinks, more simple mixed drinks, get those out of their hands and replace them with more complex cocktails. I think that at the end of the day, [our patrons are] people that have matriculated from the nightlife scene and are more interested in having more intimate, elevated experiences. What comes along with that is transitioning your palate to trying new things."

ESPRESSO EN NOIR

THE JAMES ROOM
661 AUBURN AVENUE NORTHEAST SUITE 280

The most popular cocktail right now at the James Room is the Espresso Martini, which seems to be the drink du jour both in Atlanta and beyond. It was not originally on the menu, but customers would always try to order one, so they came up with their own signature version they call the Espresso En Noir. Served in a matte-black coupe, the sexy drink tends to catch the eye, starting a wave of similar orders.

GLASSWARE: Matte-black coupe glass

GARNISH: 3 espresso beans

- 2 oz. Ketel One Vodka
- 1 oz. espresso
- ½ oz. Averna Amaro
- ½ oz. demerara syrup

1. Combine all of the ingredients in a shaker with ice, shake, then strain the cocktail into a matte-black coupe.

LOST IN TRANSLATION

THE JAMES ROOM
661 AUBURN AVENUE NORTHEAST SUITE 280

The Lost in Translation features Japanese whiskey and sake. "Those Japanese notes and Japanese flavor profiles can get literally lost in translation," Harold Brinkley says. "You don't really know what you're drinking; you just know it's good!"

GLASSWARE: Nick & Nora glass
GARNISH: Mint sprig

- 1½ oz. Suntory Whisky Toki
- ¾ oz. CHOYA Yuzu
- ¾ oz. orgeat
- ¾ oz. fresh lemon juice
- Dash Angostura bitters

1. Combine all of the ingredients in a shaker with ice, shake, then strain the cocktail into a Nick & Nora.

2. Garnish with a mint sprig.

BAR VEGAN

675 PONCE DE LEON AVENUE NORTHEAST
SUITE N-215

Pinky Cole is practically Atlanta royalty. A Clark Atlanta University graduate known best for her vegan burger chain Slutty Vegan, Cole opened the lush and green Bar Vegan in Atlanta's Ponce City Market in 2021. It's a lively spot that vegans and nonvegans alike will enjoy, with talented DJs playing hip-hop, R&B, and Afrobeats.

And then of course, Bar Vegan has a great team of bartenders.

It was the movie *Coyote Ugly* that made Bar Vegan's beverage manager, Rina Maye (pictured at left), originally want to be a bartender, because it was "so cool seeing all these women handle obnoxious men!"

For cocktail inspiration, Maye likes to pull from her Trinidadian background whenever she can. Maye also said she's found a true home working at a Black-owned establishment after a long career in the industry that is not always the most diverse. "Working here," she says, "it's not just about the craft, but the culture, being felt like I'm being understood. It's an unspoken language between my coworkers and my managers."

MARTA EXPRESS

BAR VEGAN
675 PONCE DE LEON AVENUE NORTHEAST
SUITE N-215

This drink was named Marta Express after Atlanta's rail and bus system, MARTA, which sadly is rarely "express!" Bumbu Rum is a Caribbean rum with aromas of Madagascar vanilla, caramel, and toasted oak. It's the beach in a drink!

GLASSWARE: Double rocks glass

GARNISH: Dehydrated orange, thyme leaves

- 2 oz. Bumbu Original Craft Rum
- 1 oz. fresh lime juice
- 1 oz. simple syrup
- ½ oz. pineapple juice
- ¼ oz. coconut puree

1. Combine all of the ingredients in a shaker with ice and shake.

2. Strain the cocktail into a double rocks glass with ice.

3. Garnish with a dehydrated orange and a sprig of thyme.

MO LYCHEE

BAR VEGAN
675 PONCE DE LEON AVENUE NORTHEAST
SUITE N-215

You wouldn't think lime would work with lychee, but it adds just the right amount of acidity for this lychee Martini interpretation.

GLASSWARE: Martini glass

GARNISH: Lychee fruit on a skewer

- 1½ oz. Tito's Handmade Vodka
- ½ oz. lychee puree
- ½ oz. fresh lime juice
- ½ oz. Dolin Dry Vermouth

1. Combine all of the ingredients in a shaker with ice and shake.
2. Strain the cocktail into a martini glass.
3. Garnish with a lychee fruit skewered on a cocktail pick.

KOKOMO

BAR VEGAN
675 PONCE DE LEON AVENUE NORTHEAST
SUITE N-215

The Kokomo, created by Rina Maye, goes down incredibly, almost dangerously, easy. It's absolutely refreshing, delicious, and just the right amount of sweet. The founders of Anteel Tequila, Nayana and Don Ferguson, were engaged on a beach. Maye named this tropical drink the Kokomo, from The Beach Boys song, in honor of their love story.

GLASSWARE: Martini glass

GARNISH: Sliced cucumber

- 3 to 4 slices of cucumber, muddled
- 2 oz. Anteel Coconut Lime Blanco
- 1 oz. fresh lime juice
- ½ oz. lychee puree
- ¼ oz. agave nectar

1. Combine all of the ingredients in a shaker with ice and shake.
2. Strain the cocktail into a martini glass.
3. Garnish with a sliced cucumber, floating on top.

SOUTHERN SMOKE

BAR VEGAN
675 PONCE DE LEON AVENUE NORTHEAST
SUITE N-215

Rina Maye says this mezcal drink is one of the more approachable mezcal cocktails, a great option for the first-time mezcal drinker. A Tajín side rim makes this drink extra sexy.

GLASSWARE: Double rocks glass

GARNISH: Dehydrated lime

- Tajín, for the rim
- 2 oz. Bosscal Joven Mezcal
- 1 oz. grapefruit juice
- ¾ oz. agave nectar
- ½ oz. fresh lime juice
- ½ oz. fresh lemon juice
- ½ oz. Combier Crème de Pêche de Vigne
- Ginger beer, to top

1. Wet the side of double rocks glass and roll it in Tajín powder to create a Tajín side rim.

2. Combine all of the ingredients, except for the ginger beer, in a shaker with ice and shake.

3. Strain the cocktail into the glass with more ice and top with the ginger beer.

4. Garnish with a dehydrated lime on top.

FIGGIE SMALLS

LITTLE SPIRIT
299 NORTH HIGHLAND AVENUE NORTHEAST R3

Little Spirit's Brooke Elrod made this Vieux Carre interpretation that gets fabulous fig flavor from a fig-infused cognac. To add a fun decoration on the outside of your glass like Little Spirit's cartoon, you can simply print an image of whatever you'd like onto printer paper and cut to shape. Wet the back, and it will adhere to the glass but wash off easily in the dishwasher.

GLASSWARE: Rocks glass

GARNISH: Orange peel twist, expressed

- 1 oz. Rittenhouse Straight Rye Whisky
- ¾ oz. Fig-Infused Cognac (see recipe)
- ½ oz. Cocchi Storico Vermouth di Torino
- ¼ oz. Fruitful Mission Fig Liqueur
- ¼ oz. Bénédictine
- 3 dashes Peychaud's bitters
- 2 dashes walnut bitters
- Dash Angostura bitters

1. Stir all of the ingredients in a mixing glass with ice.
2. Strain the cocktail over a big ice cube into a rocks glass. Express an orange peel over the cocktail, then add the peel as garnish.

FIG-INFUSED COGNAC: Put 1½ cups destemmed, halved figs into a mason jar and fill the jar to the top with cognac. Let it sit for 48 hours, longer for an even sweeter taste. Strain the infusion through a fine-mesh strainer then store it in an airtight bottle.

SNAP, CRACKLE, WAP

LITTLE SPIRIT
299 NORTH HIGHLAND AVENUE NORTHEAST R3

This drink, created by bartender Caroline Frese, may be a labor of love, but you can't deny that the taste and color are irresistible. It's tangy yet also creamy—a total pleasure to sip and savor. There's so much fun going on in this drink, from the playful name to the Rice Krispies Treats–infused mezcal to that vibrant purple color.

GLASSWARE: Coupe glass

GARNISH: Ube powder

- 1½ oz. Rice Krispies Treats–Infused Mezcal (see recipe)
- 1 oz. Ube Orgeat (see recipe)
- ½ oz. Hotel Tango 'Shmallow Toasted Marshmallow Bourbon
- ½ oz. Rice Milk Syrup (see recipe)
- ½ oz. fresh lemon juice
- ½ oz. fresh lime juice
- ¼ oz. St. Elizabeth Allspice Dram
- 2 dashes Bittercube Cherry Bark Vanilla Bitters
- 1 egg white

1. Build the drink in a shaker tin then dry-shake (without ice) vigorously for 30 seconds to emulsify the egg white protein.

2. Add ice and shake for 15 seconds.

3. Strain the cocktail into a coupe, top with ube powder, and swirl with a toothpick.

UBE ORGEAT: Toast 2 cups almonds, to taste, in a saucepan. Add 4 cups almond milk, 415 grams (14½ oz.) turbinado sugar, 38 grams (1⅓ oz.) ube powder, 2 tablespoons orange flower water, and 2 oz. cognac to the saucepan. Heat over medium heat until the mixture is fully combined. Remove it from heat and combine the toasted almonds and the liquid in a blender. Blend and double-strain the orgeat.

RICE MILK SYRUP: Mix equal parts rice milk and sugar in a saucepan over medium heat. Stir until the sugar is dissolved and let the syrup cool.

RICE KRISPIES TREATS–INFUSED MEZCAL: Add 4 Rice Krispies Treats per liter mezcal. Let the infusion sit overnight, blend it in a blender, then double-strain.

GROW A PEAR

LITTLE SPIRIT
299 NORTH HIGHLAND AVENUE NORTHEAST R3

I absolutely adore this drink from Little Spirit's Brooke Elrod. Sweet and delicate, Grow a Pear is aromatic, elegant, and extremely tasty. You won't be able to take just one sip, and the skeleton leaf makes an elegant garnish.

GLASSWARE: Nick & Nora glass

GARNISH: Skeleton leaf

- 1 oz. pear brandy
- 1 oz. apple soju
- ½ oz. St-Germain Elderflower Liqueur
- ½ oz. dry vermouth
- ¼ oz. Licor 43
- 2 dashes lime bitters
- 2 dashes Peychaud's bitters

1. Stir all of the ingredients together in a mixing glass with ice.
2. Strain the cocktail into a Nick & Nora.
3. Garnish with a skeleton leaf.

BURLE'S BAR

505 NORTH ANGIER AVENUE NORTHEAST SUITE 500

Burle's Bar is actually pronounced "burly," but beverage director Andrew Selvagn wouldn't blame you if you said it wrong. (Everyone does.) Nestled in the upstairs loft of popular plant shop The Victorian Atlanta, Burle's Bar is befittingly named after Roberto Burle Marx. Marx was a Brazilian naturalist credited with unearthing over fifty varieties of plants, of which many are sold today as houseplants.

Selvagn teamed up with husband-and-wife duo Libby Hockenberry and Cary Smith to open up Burle's Bar. What was once a blank space has been transformed into a verdant green oasis: brushed green walls, checkerboard green floors, green bar tiles, green marble, green plants, and green chairs. The overall effect is an incredibly soothing 1960s-inspired bar that perhaps unsurprisingly attracts a calmer, slightly older crowd than BeltLine bars are typically used to seeing. Beyond aesthetics, they make great drinks.

Selvagn takes a classic approach to cocktails. (Call him a bartender, not a mixologist.) He argues that we don't need to reinvent the wheel, but just polish it up a bit. Perfect execution, not pretension, is what he strives for, and at a reasonable price. Here, cocktails aren't given cheeky names, but simply called what they've always been called throughout history, which he says helps clear up confusion from guests.

"It's all been done before," he says. "You go around, and it's like a twelve-ingredient cocktail, with a stupid name, then you gotta sound like an asshole ordering it."

The spirits at his bar are sourced ethically and intentionally. Nothing artificial and no sketchy labor practices, which he notes is particularly crucial when you look into procuring rum. Selvagn's ultimate aim for Burle's Bar was to create a place he would want to hang out in, where you feel as comfortable ordering a $3 Miller High Life as you would a Bijou. The menu includes a dedicated section for beer and shots. "To have an awesome cocktail doesn't mean you have to have a stuffy environment," he says. Burle's Bar proves that you can find that sweet middle ground between a dive and an ultra-swanky cocktail lounge. The effect is enchanting.

THREE DOTS & A DASH

BURLE'S BAR
505 NORTH ANGIER AVENUE NORTHEAST SUITE 500

It's not as famous as the Mai Tai, but the Three Dots & a Dash is a fantastic tiki drink to add to your repertoire. It was created during WWII, and its name is morse code for the letter V for "Victor." At Burle's Bar, the ginger-honey syrup is house-made, the ratios are tweaked a bit, and the overall effect is a drink that's a little more autumnal than the original.

GLASSWARE: Collins glass

GARNISH: 3 cherries on a skewer, dehydrated lime wheel

- 1¼ oz. Rhum J.M Blanc
- 1 oz. Chairman's Reserve Original Rum
- ½ oz. Ginger-Honey Syrup (see recipe)
- ½ oz. fresh lime juice
- ½ oz. fresh orange juice
- ¼ oz. St. Elizabeth Allspice Dram
- ¼ oz. Luau Lads Falernum
- 10 drops tiki bitters
- 2 dashes Angostura bitters
- 6 drops Saline Solution (see recipe on page 195)

1. Shake all of the ingredients together with ice in a cocktail shaker.

2. Strain the cocktail into a collins glass over pebble ice or crushed ice.

3. Garnish with 3 skewered cherries and a dehydrated lime wheel.

GINGER-HONEY SYRUP: In a saucepan over medium-low heat, combine 5 oz. honey and ½ oz. water and bring to a simmer, stirring. Add ½ oz. ginger juice and immediately cut off the heat. Allow the syrup to cool.

BIJOU

BURLE'S BAR
505 NORTH ANGIER AVENUE NORTHEAST SUITE 500

Bijou is spirit-forward but also super palatable. The bermutto is the secret. It's a vermouth made with sake that pulls in yuzu and wormwood notes—not technically a vermouth, but the Japanese call it so. Burle's Bar serves it in an elegant glass that's somewhat of a hybrid between a martini glass and a Nick & Nora.

GLASSWARE: Martini glass

GARNISH: Lemon channel peel

- 1½ oz. Tanqueray N° Ten Gin
- ¾ oz. Tsutsumi Distillery Bermutto
- ½ oz. Green Chartreuse
- 2 dashes Scrappy's Black Lemon Bitters

1. Add all of the ingredients into a mixing glass with ice, stir, and double-strain the cocktail into a martini glass.

2. Garnish with a lemon channel peel.

ESPRESSO MARTINI

Like many bartenders around Atlanta, Andrew Salzceman was somewhat bullied into making an Espresso Martini at the request of customers repeatedly trying to order it despite it not being listed on the menu. Eventually, he acquiesced and sought to make the best one he could make. A fat-washed tequila makes this drink creamy and delicious.

GLASSWARE: Coupe glass

GARNISH: Nutmeg, microplaned

- 1½ oz. cold brew espresso
- ¾ oz. Coconut Fat–Washed Tequila (see recipe)
- ¾ oz. Brandy Sainte Louise
- ½ oz. St. George NOLA Coffee Liqueur
- ¼ oz. Faretti Biscotti Liqueur
- ¼ oz. cinnamon syrup

1. Shake all of the ingredients together in a cocktail shaker with ice.
2. Double-strain the cocktail into a coupe, then microplane nutmeg over the top to garnish.

COCONUT FAT–WASHED TEQUILA: Use a 5:1 ratio of Arette Blanco Tequila to coconut oil. Heat the oil so it's liquified and then combine the ingredients and stir. Let the infusion sit at room temperature for a few hours before putting it in the refrigerator. Pull it out 24 hours later, remove the solidified oil, strain, and rebottle the tequila.

SOUTHSIDE

BURLE'S BAR
505 NORTH ANGIER AVENUE NORTHEAST SUITE 500

This drink rocks. It's an interpretation of the classic cocktail the Southside, but almost everything is different. It's served in a rocks glass with ice instead of a coupe. The ratios are different. And it's supremely sippable and refreshing.

GLASSWARE: Rocks glass

GARNISH: Mint sprig

- 1½ oz. Murrell's Row Tulsi Gin
- ¾ oz. fresh lemon juice
- ½ oz. Sipsmith VJOP Gin
- ½ oz. simple syrup
- ¼ oz. Green Chartreuse
- Dash grapefruit bitters
- 6 mint leaves
- Lemon peel, to express

1. Combine all of the ingredients, except for the lemon peel, in a cocktail shaker and shake.

2. Double-strain the cocktail into a rocks glass with ice.

3. Express a lemon peel over the drink then discard the peel. Garnish with a mint sprig.

TIMOTHY PARKER, ELECTRIC HOSPITALITY

Timothy Parker is the beverage director for Electric Hospitality, where he oversees upwards of sixty-five bartenders across three concepts. Ladybird is a campy backyard-hangout spot on Atlanta's BeltLine; Ranger Station is a cocktail bar with hunting lodge vibes nestled in Ladybird's upstairs loft; and lastly, Muchacho is a casual Reynoldstown restaurant with excellent coffee, agave-based cocktails, and breakfast burritos.

Do you have a favorite ingredient you like to incorporate in your cocktails?

Rum. Rum. Rum! Rum. Rum. Rum. R-u-m, r-h-u-m, r-h-o-n, any of them all, all the sugarcane spirits of the world. That is my favorite thing, I love it. A lot of people in their houses have decanters of, you know, crazy rare spirits. I always have a really nice crystal canter of $21-a-liter Jamaican jet fuel. Yes, rum!

It's like wine. It is so different: there's terroir to it, there's technique to it, there's history to it. So many people are taking rum production seriously right now. You can get unbelievably cool rum at an unbelievable value. More people should try more rum, all the time.

I feel like Ladybird was one the first ones in Atlanta to have those "Capri Sun" drinks served in a plastic pouch.

That was a COVID necessity, actually. We needed to be able to give people something that they didn't necessarily have to drink at the bar. We had some really smart people thinking about, "What is the way we can get stuff in people's hands? Still give people jobs, and still provide something for people?" During COVID, for a lot of people a glass of wine or a cocktail were peak enjoyment because it was such a brutal time.

Ladybird has been reformatted a couple of times because it has just taken on this life of its own. Ladybird is peak hangout, enjoy the vibe of a beautiful outside space, very well-done inside space, but it is a hangout. It is a lot of people coming all the time to enjoy what we have going on. So Ladybird is, how do we do stuff at high volume?

How many customers do you see on a typical 70-degree Saturday at Ladybird?

I mean, I think with people, our capacity is right around 1,300 and we will stay at capacity with people flowing in and out from 2 p.m. to 7 p.m. So you're probably looking at close to 7,000 or 8,000 bar transactions. We're selling 3,000 seltzers in a can. We're selling those Capri Sun pouches, which we call patio pouches, probably all together 1,200 of those on a Saturday, if not more.

And then for Ranger Station, which is more of the opposite side, what does your approach look like?

So, the idea of Ranger Station is that in a lot of ways, it feels like the opposite, but really what we wanted to do was concentrate Ladybird. So it's like, what's the quintessence of Ladybird? Ranger Station is

definitely a cocktail bar. It is a place where we are making very well-done, very well executed, very thoughtful cocktails, and that's the big part. We have great food, but people are coming there to get a really, really well-done cocktail menu. And I will say that that is a great example of collaborative effort, because we have Tom Kastanowski, who is our beverage there, and he works year-round on R&D, R&D, and R&D.

But, because Ladybird is 100% about hanging out, having a good time, partying your heart out kind of vibe, we wanted Ranger Station to be a cocktail bar that wasn't so self-serious that you couldn't have a good time.

We love the idea of doing cool things, we're adults up here, but we're absolutely going to cut loose, be boisterous, be a little rowdy, have a good time. We want you to be able to come in and treat your friends to the best cocktail they've ever had, but also feel really good about ordering a beer and a shot. We don't want you to worry if you laugh too loud or talk too much or anything like that.

But this is a place where we're not scared to take a little bit longer, have multiple touches on a cocktail, have a lot of different preparations, lots of specific glassware, actually curate a cocktail experience not just through product but through service as well. It's a little more high-end, but still super fun and very accessible.

Any advice for someone at home who's maybe picking up this book and maybe wanting to try to make some of these cocktails at home?

I think people are either entirely too casual or entirely too serious in their approach to making drinks, and I think the answer is neither one of those. Literally, I've shaken drinks at parties in Tupperware containers. You can church it up all you want to, but at the end of the day we're making a drink. We're trying to have something that makes you want to party a little bit. Number one, always have a little party in your heart!

This is about conviviality; this is about bringing people together, relaxing, chilling out, having a good time. When you're having a good time, it's really hard to go wrong.

Muchacho (see also page 203)

EL CAPITAN

RANGER STATION
684 JOHN WESLEY DOBBS AVENUE NORTHEAST UNIT J

The Gimlet gets a more herbaceous feel to it with Ranger Station's El Capitan, named after the cliff in Yosemite National Park.

GLASSWARE: Nick & Nora glass

GARNISH: Sage leaf

- 2 oz. Sage & Cardamom–Infused Gin (see recipe)
- 1 oz. Pineapple Puree (see recipe)
- ¾ oz. fresh lemon juice
- ½ oz. Clove Demerara Syrup (see recipe)

1. Combine all of the ingredients with ice in a cocktail shaker, shake hard, then fine-strain the cocktail into a Nick & Nora.

SAGE AND CARDAMOM–INFUSED GIN: Put 1 liter gin, 38 grams torn fresh sage, and 5 grams cracked green cardamom into an airtight container and let the mixture infuse for 24 hours. Strain and bottle.

PINEAPPLE PUREE: Peel and core a pineapple. Blend the flesh of the pineapple until smooth.

CLOVE DEMERARA SYRUP: Toast 25 grams cloves until fragrant, 1 to 2 minutes. Add 500 grams water, 500 grams demerara sugar, and the cloves to a saucepan and cook on medium-low heat for 30 minutes, stirring constantly. Allow the syrup to cool, then strain and bottle. Shake hard before using.

TRUTH AND CONSEQUENCES

RANGER STATION
684 JOHN WESLEY DOBBS AVENUE NORTHEAST UNIT J

Mexican verdita brings an herbal flavor to tequila. Lime adds acidity, and cinnamon even more fragrance and sweetness.

GLASSWARE: Collins glass

GARNISH: Mint, pineapple wedge

- 2 oz. blanco tequila
- 1½ oz. Verdita (see recipe)
- ¾ oz. fresh lime juice
- ½ oz. Cinnamon Syrup (see recipe)

1. Combine all of the ingredients in a cocktail shaker with ice, shake, and strain the cocktail into a collins glass.

VERDITA: Put 1 liter pineapple juice, 1 whole jalepeño, and 140 grams fresh mint into a blender. Blend until smooth. Strain and bottle.

CINNAMON SYRUP: Break up 5 cassia cinnamon sticks into pieces and toast until fragrant. Add the cinnamon sticks, 250 grams water, and 250 grams sugar to a saucepan and cook on medium-low heat for 30 minutes, stirring constantly. Let the syrup cool, strain, and bottle.

LIFE OF LEISURE

684 JOHN WESLEY DOBBS AVENUE NORTHEAST UNIT J

Tequila, Tajín, and pineapple always go perfectly together, especially when enjoyed on the patio of Ladybird.

GLASSWARE: Rocks glass

GARNISH: Pineapple fronds, pineapple wedge, Tajín

- 2 oz. blanco tequila
- ½ oz. Martini Fiero
- ½ oz. Clement Mahina Coco
- 1 oz. pineapple juice
- ½ oz. fresh lime juice
- ¼ oz. agave nectar

1. Combine all of the ingredients in a cocktail shaker and shake with ice.
2. Strain the cocktail into a rocks glass.
3. Garnish with a pineapple wedge and a sprinkle of Tajín.

LAID BACK

LADYBIRD
684 JOHN WESLEY DOBBS AVENUE NORTHEAST UNIT J

Rum, bourbon, the French herbal liqueur Bénédictine, and cream sherry make for an unusual mix that, when combined, create cocktail magic.

GLASSWARE: Rocks glass

GARNISH: Lemon peel

- 1 oz. bourbon
- ½ oz. spiced rum
- ¼ oz. cream sherry
- ¼ oz. Bénédictine
- ¼ oz. simple syrup
- 2 dashes Angostura bitters

1. Combine all of the ingredients and shake with ice.

2. Strain the cocktail into a rocks glass.

3. Garnish with a lemon peel.

FRANCIS COLIGADO, DELBAR

Delbar, which means "heart, captured" in Farsi, is one of Atlanta's most popular Persian and Middle Eastern restaurants. On any given night, it's bustling with packed dinner tables and a lively energy, even nabbing a mention in the coveted *Michelin Guide* in 2023.

Francis Coligado, a seasoned bartender with seventeen years of experience, is the force driving their impressive beverage program.

For Coligado, being behind the bar is more than a profession. It's an opportunity to express his true self. "I love giving my guests a great experience and providing them with a good time; it just speaks to my soul, really," he shares.

Coligado has carefully curated a balanced menu at Delbar, with a thoughtful selection of refreshing and lighter drinks to counteract some of the richness of Delbar's food as well as more spirit-forward offerings.

When it comes to drink inspiration, Coligado says he pulls from everywhere.

For Delbar's signature drinks, he frequently works with cinnamon, star anise, cardamom, and "so many herbs."

Then a lot of the time, his inspirations will be culinary-driven, trying to replicate some of the flavors in a great dish into a drink.

His childhood is also a rich well to pull from: "Nostalgia's a big one, like strawberry shortcake ice creams from the gas stations; there was one time I made a cocktail trying to replicate those flavors," he says.

Then on the rare occasion, Coligado will "be walking down the BeltLine, I'll see a cool painting, and the colors will speak to me. Sometimes I don't even have any flavors to start out with; I just already know what it's going to look like," he explains.

PINEAPPLE PURPLE SKY

Delbar's beverage director Francis Coligado likes to, in his time away from Delbar's Middle Eastern–focused menu, pull in flavors and influences from his Filipino heritage. To whit: this ube concoction.

GLASSWARE: Collins glass

GARNISH: Basil leaf

- 1 oz. Tanduay Silver Asian Rum
- 1 oz. La Luna Mezcal
- ½ oz. Giffard Banane du Brésil
- ¾ oz. Ube Coconut Cream (see recipe)
- 1 oz. pineapple juice
- ½ oz. fresh lime juice

1. Combine all of the ingredients and shake hard with ice, then pour the cocktail into a collins glass.

2. Garnish with a basil leaf.

UBE COCONUT CREAM: In a container, mix together 12 oz. coconut cream, 6 oz. simple syrup, and 1 teaspoon ube extract until fully incorporated.

SAUDI MONEY

DELBAR
870 INMAN VILLAGE PARKWAY NORTHEAST SUITE 1

A Middle Eastern staple, tart cherry is the sweetener for this delightfully boozy, bourbon drink from Delbar's beverage director, Francis Coligado. A touch of gold leaf elegantly placed onto a maraschino cherry adds an impossibly stylish flair. You can find tart (also called sour cherry) syrup at Middle Eastern grocery stores.

GLASSWARE: Highball glass

GARNISH: Gold leaf cherry

- 1½ oz. Old Forester Bourbon 100
- ¾ oz. fresh lime juice
- ¾ oz. tart cherry syrup
- ⅕ oz. Amaro CioCiaro

1. Combine all of the ingredients in a mixing glass and stir.
2. Pour the cocktail into a rocks glass with one large ice cube.
3. Garnish with a speared cherry adorned with a touch of gold leaf.

DUBAI DRIFT

DELBAR
870 INMAN VILLAGE PARKWAY NORTHEAST SUITE 1

Chai spice and maple are an irresistible combination with Japanese whiskey in this drink that just screams autumn. A barspoon of soy lecithin solution helps add frothiness. Finally, star anise adds even more fall fragrance to this drink, and looks picture perfect in a Nick & Nora glass.

GLASSWARE: Nick & Nora glass

GARNISH: Star anise pod

- 1 oz. Suntory Whisky Toki
- 1 oz. Calvados
- ½ oz. Chai Spice Ginger Syrup (see recipe)

- ½ oz. maple syrup
- 1 oz. fresh lime juice
- Barspoon soy lecithin solution

1. Combine all of the ingredients in a shaker then shake hard to combine.

2. Strain the cocktail into a Nick & Nora.

3. Garnish with star anise.

CHAI SPICE GINGER SYRUP: Put 500 grams chopped ginger, 4 cups water, 10 grams cardamom, 15 grams black peppercorns, and 5 grams star anise into a blender and mix. Fine-strain the mixture into a fresh container. Weigh the remaining liquid, add an equal amount of water, and stir until fully dissolved.

NORTH ATLANTA SUBURBS AND NEIGHBORHOODS

IN BLOOM	CUCUMBER MARTINI
A GLIMMER OF HOPS	GOLDEN HOUR
GÉNÉPY MARGARITA	RUM DRANK
THE THIRD DOOR'S ESPRESSO MARTINI	THE GRANTHAM
	CIDER CIPHER (NA)
CLARK, GET ME A STOGIE	SUMMERTIME SETBACK
BEARCAT (NA)	TEQUILA OLD FASHIONED
SPICY CRANBERRY MARGARITA	SPANISH PIPEDREAM
LEMONGRASS + 18.21 LEMON BASIL	PLOT TWIST
	BULLS EYE
REDEMPTION RYE + 18.21 APPLE CARDAMOM SHRUB	BITTERSWEET SYMPHONY
SIDECAR	IT'S STRAWBERRY THYME
ANGEL'S SHARE	SWEATER WEATHER
NIGHT SKY	TO "QUILA" MOCKINGBIRD
	RUSH HOUR
WHAT THE KIDS CALL FIRE	FILTHY OLD FASHIONED

Before I get a ton of hate from locals for including these spots in this book, let me just get out in front of it.

Is Duluth Atlanta? No. Is Sandy Springs Atlanta? No.

But they *are* part of the Greater Metro Atlanta area, and I'm here to inform you that they absolutely *do* have restaurants and bars serving up excellent cocktails that are more than worth the drive.

So, are we good with that? Alright? Good.

Now, hop in your car and let's explore some of the best drinks that Atlanta's northern suburbs have to offer.

Local fun fact: Much of Atlanta burned down in 1864 when Union forces stormed the city during the Civil War, which means that there are few historical buildings in Atlanta proper. However, you can still find many pre–Civil War structures in northern suburbs like Roswell and Norcross.

DISTILLERY OF MODERN ART

2197 IRVINDALE DRIVE, CHAMBLEE

The Distillery of Modern Art has to be one of the Atlanta area's most unique drinking establishments. After a long and fruitful career in planning events, spanning everything from 200-person weddings to the Chick-fil-A Peach Bowl, distillery founder Seth Watson (pictured opposite, at left) decided he wanted to create memorable experiences around his passion for craft spirits. The result is a continually growing line of affordable and approachable locally made spirits in a beautiful modern art gallery—the Distillery of Modern Art.

A lot of research and planning went into making his dream come true. "The state of Georgia has a lot of holdover laws from Prohibition that made it difficult to manufacture alcohol," says Watson. As a result, the Distillery of Modern Art is one of only a single-digit number of active liquor distilleries in the Atlanta metro area.

Watson views the Distillery of Modern Art as a part of a wave of Atlanta's ever-improving cocktail culture. "We're long away from the days of the back bar being filled with weird-flavored, overly sugary, syrupy, chemically flavored liqueurs," he says. "Customers now seek more from their brands and their experiences." That translates to an emphasis on making things from scratch: "We make all of our juices, all of our syrups, all of our tinctures, everything, in-house. Our garnishes are grown in the garden and used on top of our cocktails, and our menus change seasonally."

Is it any surprise then that their most popular offerings infuse local flavors—most notably, Georgia's most famous export, the peach? The Distillery of Modern Art's peach vodka beautifully sets itself apart from other more typically artificially flavored vodkas on the market by infusing real Georgia peaches, apricot, and orange blossoms.

Their second-best seller is a liqueur—an herbaceous peach-flavored amaro. Amaro, which directly translates to "bitter" from Italian, is traditionally more of a sharp after-dinner drink that is supposed to promote

digestion after a heavy meal. The distillery turns its nose up at tradition and instead has created an amaro that's a little more approachable to American palates, an impossibly good blend that Watson describes as somehow "deep and rich and sweet and bitter." A wonderful way to enjoy it is as a nightcap with just a squeeze of citrus in it.

But what may be the Distillery's most unique selling point is that not only can you enjoy fabulous cocktails with made-in-Georgia ingredients in their beautiful and modern cocktail lounge, but you can also view and experience rotating art installations created by some of Atlanta's talented creatives and artists. The art on display is available to take home for purchase, and the Distillery takes no commissions from its artists. "Everything has to have a component that gives back," says Watson.

IN BLOOM

Bar manager Trey Jones considers the In Bloom his signature cocktail. "It's gorgeous," he says, "but, looking at the ingredients, you wouldn't expect it to have the flavor that it does. With the bitters, you get an herbaceous note, and it finishes with a bittersweet and really bright finish." When Trey is going for a holiday vibe, he supplements the leaf garnish with red marigolds picked fresh from the distillery's garden.

GLASSWARE: Nick & Nora glass

GARNISH: Nasturtium leaf, red marigolds (optional)

- 1½ oz. Distillery of Modern Art Amaro Peach
- ¾ oz. Tempus Fugit Crème de Menthe
- ½ oz. citric acid
- ½ oz. simple syrup
- 4 dashes Bittermens Transatlantic Modern Aromatic Bitters

1. Combine all of the ingredients together in a cocktail shaker with ice and shake thoroughly.

2. Double-strain the cocktail into a Nick & Nora and garnish with a nasturtium leaf and, if using, red marigolds.

A GLIMMER OF HOPS

Citrus, thyme, and the distillery's bestselling peach-flavored vodka take center stage in this hoppy drink.

GLASSWARE: Highball glass

GARNISH: Thyme sprig

- 1½ oz. Distillery of Modern Art Peach-Flavored Vodka
- 1 oz. Cascade Hops Tea (see recipe)
- 1 oz. grapefruit juice
- ½ oz. simple syrup
- ½ oz. lemon juice
- 2 grapefruit slices
- Club soda, to top

1. Combine the vodka, tea, grapefruit juice, simple syrup, and lemon juice in a cocktail shaker with ice and shake.

2. Double-strain the cocktail into an ice-filled highball lined with grapefruit slices.

3. Garnish with a thyme sprig and top with soda.

CASCADE HOPS TEA: Combine 1 gram hops and 500 ml boiling water and steep for 25 minutes. Strain out the hops and allow the tea to cool.

THE THIRD DOOR

131 CHURCH STREET, MARIETTA

What may very well be Atlanta's coolest speakeasy is not in Atlanta at all, but just northwest of the city in the sleepier Marietta suburbs. The Third Door's husband-and-wife owners, Ted and Lara Ferreira, converted an old gas station into a rockin' Prohibition-style cocktail bar. The mood is set by glamorous tin tiles adorning the ceiling, a beautiful and rustic bar made from reclaimed pine wood from the 1920s, and tons of outdoor seating, perfect for enjoying a drink in fair Atlanta weather.

It's no surprise that the man behind the bar, Jonátan (Joná) Ruiz, is as impossibly cool as The Third Door is. Originally from Ciudad Obregón in Mexico, Ruiz grew up in Tennessee but went back to Mexico for college, where got his start in the food and beverage industry while studying for his history degree. Interestingly, Ruiz says it was actually the storied history of the Prohibition era in the U.S. that first sparked his interest in the cocktail world. "If you come to my house, I have a bunch of books on cocktails and the history of specific spirits. It's an interesting world, the craft cocktail world; you find people from all walks of life," says Ruiz.

The Third Door focuses on classic Prohibition-era cocktails, so Ruiz works a lot with amaros, liqueurs, and gins while adding a modern twist to each drink. However, he does love to draw inspiration from his Mexican background and his years growing up in Tennessee wherever it is appropriate. Bourbon is a favorite ingredient of his, and The Third Door has a curated array of agave spirits as well. The "Clark, Get Me A Stoagie" on The Third Door's holiday menu incorporates both agave spirits and Mexican flavors.

Two very different drinks are among The Third Door's most popular offerings: the house Negroni and the house Margarita. The Negroni sources an excellent sweet vermouth, Cocchi Storico Vermouth di Torino, and a one-year barrel-aged gin called Bristow from a craft distillery in Mississippi. Ruiz puts a brilliant spin on the Margarita that adds a Prohibition-era glamour: the French herbal liqueur génépy in place of triple sec or orange liqueur.

Ruiz is newer to the Atlanta metro area, but he's already a big fan and big believer in our mixology future. "There's still more to come," he says. "We're growing and every time we see a list of best bars in the U.S., there's always one or two of them from Atlanta, and I do think in the near future we're going to have more representation on the national and international stage as well."

GÉNÉPY MARGARITA

THE THIRD DOOR
131 CHURCH STREET, MARIETTA

I t's hard to improve upon the much-beloved Margarita, but the addition of herbaceous génépy may very well do the trick.

GLASSWARE: Rocks glass

GARNISH: Dehydrated lemon

- 2 oz. Pueblo Viejo Blanco Tequila
- ½ oz. Dolin Génépy le Chamois Liqueur
- ¾ oz. fresh lime juice
- ¼ oz. agave nectar
- 2 dashes orange bitters

1. Combine all of the ingredients and shake with ice, then strain the cocktail into a rocks glass.

2. Garnish with a dehydrated lemon.

THE THIRD DOOR'S ESPRESSO MARTINI

THE THIRD DOOR
131 CHURCH STREET, MARIETTA

Having a killer Espresso Martini is a must on any menu these days, and The Third Door's Joná Ruiz puts his spin on it by incorporating sherry and chicory liqueur.

GLASSWARE: Coupe glass

GARNISH: 3 espresso beans

- 1¼ oz. Cathead Vodka
- 1 oz. Tuesday's Coffee Shop Concentrated Cold Brew
- ½ oz. Luxardo Coffee Liqueur
- ¼ oz. Giffard Vanille de Madagascar
- ¼ oz. Hoodoo Chicory Liqueur
- ¼ oz. Lustau East India Cream Sherry
- Dash Fee Brothers Fee Foam
- Dash lemon bitters

1. Combine all of the ingredients and shake with ice, then strain the cocktail into a coupe glass.
2. Garnish with 3 espresso beans.

CLARK, GET ME A STOGIE

THE THIRD DOOR
131 CHURCH STREET, MARIETTA

Atlanta loves a Christmas pop-up bar, and The Third Door crafted a Christmas signature menu with this excellent drink that infuses a taste of Mexico at Christmastime. It's a delightfully boozy drink, so sip it slowly. Caramel popcorn makes for a fun garnish.

GLASSWARE: Rocks glass

GARNISH: Spray of mezcal, 3 caramel corn popcorn kernels on a cocktail pick

- 1½ oz. Pueblo Viejo Reposado Tequila
- ½ oz. Tanteo Navidad Tequila
- ¼ oz. Fratello Hazelnut Liqueur
- ¼ oz. Nixta Licor de Elote
- ¼ oz. Orange Juice Syrup (see recipe)
- 2 dashes Bittermens Xocolatl Mole Bitters

1. Combine all of the ingredients in a mixing glass and stir.

2. Pour the cocktail into a rocks glass and garnish with a mezcal spray and caramel popcorn.

ORANGE JUICE SYRUP: Heat together a 1:1 ratio of orange juice and white sugar in a saucepan, stirring until the sugar has dissolved.

BEARCAT (NA)

THE THIRD DOOR
131 CHURCH STREET, MARIETTA

Nonalcoholic drinks are having a moment in Atlanta, for both the nondrinkers as well as those who are simply looking to be a bit more health conscious. The Third Door makes a refreshing aloe-and-cucumber drink with a touch of the always-pleasing ginger beer.

GLASSWARE: Rocks glass

GARNISH: 3 cucumber coins speared on a cocktail pick

- **3 slices of cucumber, muddled**
- **1 oz. Lyre's Dry London Spirit**
- **1 oz. aloe vera juice**
- **½ oz. fresh lime juice**
- **½ oz. simple syrup**
- **Ginger beer, to top**

1. In a cocktail shaker, shake all of the ingredients, except for the ginger beer, with ice, then strain the cocktail into a rocks glass.

2. Top with ginger beer. Gently stir with a barspoon to mix.

3. Garnish with 3 cucumber coins on a cocktail pick.

18.21 BITTERS

1927 LAKESIDE PARKWAY, TUCKER

Missy and Kristin Koefod are the visionary duo behind the much-beloved 18.21 Bitters in Atlanta. Named for the eighteenth amendment outlawing alcohol and the twenty-first amendment repealing it, 18.21's genesis began when the couple came up with a few bitters recipes while stuck inside during Atlanta's 2014 ice storm (known here as "Snowpocalypse"), which shut down the city for days.

18.21 started with just premium bitters, which are flavor extracts infused with botanicals (herbs and spices) that make any cocktail exponentially better. Missy describes them as the "spice rack for your cocktails." But it wasn't long before 18.21 expanded into a line of incredible shrubs, syrups, tinctures, and even tonic and ginger beer.

In the decade since its inception, 18.21 has become synonymous with Atlanta's vibrant cocktail culture, gracing the menus of numerous establishments across the city. Yet, their influence extends far beyond the peach state, with their products embraced in forty-eight states, six countries, and counting. It's a testament to the duo's unwavering commitment to crafting exceptional libations.

PREMIUM
18·21
BITTERS
CRAFTING A BETTER COCKTAIL
COCKTA
CRAFTED IN ATLANTA GE
BATCH No.
16 fl oz (473 mL)

SPICY CRANBERRY MARGARITA

18.21 BITTERS
1927 LAKESIDE PARKWAY, TUCKER

I n a city as hot as Atlanta, a cold holiday beverage like this Margarita is perfect for those 60 degree December days. Combine a few cranberries and sprigs of rosemary in an ice cube tray for big ice cubes to go the extra mile on presentation.

GLASSWARE: Rocks glass

GARNISH: Rosemary, blood orange, cranberries

- 2 oz. blanco tequila
- 8 drops 18.21 Japanese Chili and Lime Bitters
- ¾ oz. blood orange juice
- ¾ oz. 18.21 Holiday Syrup
- Himalayan sea salt, for the rim
- Sugar, for the rim

1. Shake all of the ingredients, except for the sugar and salt, in a cocktail shaker well over ice.

2. Strain the cocktail into a rocks glass with a salt and sugar rim.

3. Garnish with rosemary, blood orange, and cranberries.

LEMONGRASS + 18.21 LEMON BASIL

18.21 BITTERS
1927 LAKESIDE PARKWAY, TUCKER

Lemongrass, yuzu, and coconut water make for a perfect blend of Asian flavors that all come together for a refreshing drink.

GLASSWARE: Rocks glass
GARNISH: Kaffir lime leaf

- 1½ oz. vodka
- 1 oz. coconut water
- ½ oz. 18.21 Lemon Basil Syrup
- ½ oz. fresh lime juice
- ½ oz. lemongrass moringa tea
- 18.21 Yuzu Herb Tonic, to top

1. In a cocktail shaker with ice, shake the vodka, coconut water, syrup, lime juice, and tea.

2. Strain the cocktail into a rocks glass and top with the tonic.

3. Garnish with a Kaffir lime leaf and serve with a straw.

REDEMPTION RYE + 18.21 APPLE CARDAMOM SHRUB

18.21 BITTERS
1927 LAKESIDE PARKWAY, TUCKER

A cardamom shrub and an herbal simple syrup combine with rye to bring you autumn in a glass. Be sure to go all out with the presentation of your garnish and ice.

GLASSWARE: Rocks glass

GARNISH: Smoked rosemary, black pepper

- 2 oz. Redemption Rye Whiskey
- ½ oz. 18.21 Apple Cardamom Shrub
- ½ oz. rosemary sage syrup
- ½ oz. Cardamaro
- ½ oz. fresh lemon juice

1. In a cocktail shaker with ice, shake all of the ingredients well.

2. Strain the cocktail into a rocks glass over a large ice cube.

3. Garnish with smoked rosemary and black pepper.

SIDECAR

Roswell is one of Atlanta's most picturesque suburbs, with an abundance of historic homes and lively, walkable streets filled with great restaurants and bars. 1920 Tavern was started by a South African husband-and-wife duo, and has over the years built quite an extensive cocktail menu that includes seven different spins on the Old Fashioned. While Old Fashioneds are 1920 Tavern's most popular drink, their Sidecar is also well loved and is made with a premium bourbon instead of cognac.

GLASSWARE: Coupe glass

GARNISH: Lemon twist

- Brown sugar, for the rim
- 2 oz. Eagle Rare 10 Year

- 1 oz. Combier Liqueur D'orange
- ½ oz. fresh lemon juice

1. Wet half of the rim of a coupe then dip it in brown sugar to give the glass a half rim.

2. Mix the remaining ingredients together in a mixing glass.

3. Pour the cocktail into the coupe and garnish with a lemon twist.

ANGEL'S SHARE

Angel Gomez at Branch & Barrel created this cocktail. He incorporates a high-rye bourbon that can stand up against the other ingredients. This drink is called the Angel's Share, which serves a dual purpose since the bartender's name is Angel and the "angel's share" refers to the whiskey that evaporates out of whiskey barrels during the aging process.

GLASSWARE: Rocks glass

GARNISH: Dehydrated lemon wheel, rosemary

- 2 oz. Basil Hayden Bourbon
- 1 oz. cranberry juice
- 1 oz. Rosemary Simple Syrup (see recipe)
- ½ oz. fresh lemon juice

1. Shake all of the ingredients in a cocktail shaker with ice.

2. Strain the cocktail into a rocks glass with fresh ice, then garnish with a dehydrated lemon wheel and rosemary. You can smoke the end of the rosemary for added aroma and effect.

ROSEMARY SIMPLE SYRUP: Add 2 cups sugar and 2 cups hot water to a container. Whisk until the sugar is dissolved. Then add rosemary sprigs, to taste. Steep for 20 minutes, then remove the rosemary.

NIGHT SKY

BRANCH & BARREL
4100 AVALON BOULEVARD, ALPHARETTA

The Night Sky is a riff on an Aviation and a Bee's Knees. At Branch & Barrel, they like to use Georgi London Dry Gin, but you can ultimately use whichever gin you like.

GLASSWARE: Coupe glass

GARNISH: Dehydrated lemon wheel

- 2 oz. Georgi London Dry Gin
- ¾ oz. fresh lemon juice
- ½ oz. Combier Liqueur de Violette
- ½ oz. Fruitful Blackberry Liqueur
- ½ oz. Honey Syrup (see recipe)
- 2 dashes Fee Brothers Grapefruit Bitters

1. Shake all of the ingredients in a cocktail shaker with ice.
2. Strain the cocktail into a coupe and garnish with a dehydrated lemon wheel.

HONEY SYRUP: Add 2 cups clover honey and 1 cup hot water to a container and whisk until combined.

WHAT THE KIDS CALL FIRE

BRANCH & BARREL
4100 AVALON BOULEVARD, ALPHARETTA

Bar manager Taylor Smith got his start in hospitality at the age of 13, when he had to pitch in one day at his dad's restaurant and help with dishwashing. At Branch & Barrel, he's curated a menu of thirteen signature cocktails. Taylor says the garnish is edible and "tastes like a spicy key lime pie." When you dehydrate lime, it can take a lot of the sour flavor out of it, so it's much less bitter than you'd expect.

GLASSWARE: Rocks glass

GARNISH: Dehydrated lime wheel with Tajín

- Tajín, for the rim
- 2 oz. Habanero-Infused Mezcal (see recipe)
- 1 oz. Bell Pepper & Jalapeño Shrub (see recipe)
- 1 oz. fresh lime juice
- ½ oz. pineapple juice
- ½ oz. agave nectar

1. Wet the rim of a rocks glass and dip the glass in Tajín to rim the glass.

2. Shake all of the ingredients in a cocktail shaker with ice.

3. Strain the cocktail into the rocks glass over fresh ice and garnish with a dehydrated lime wheel with Tajín.

HABANERO-INFUSED MEZCAL: Chop 3 to 4 habanero peppers into quarters, add them to a container, seeds and all, with 1 (750 ml) bottle of 400 Conejos Joven Espadín Mezcal and let it sit for 20 to 30 minutes, depending on how hot you'd like it. Strain the mezcal through a fine-mesh strainer

BELL PEPPER & JALAPEÑO SHRUB: Remove the seeds from 4 green bell peppers and 2 jalapeño peppers and blend the peppers until smooth. Transfer the mixture to a pot, add 4 cups sugar and 4 cups white vinegar, stirring to combine. Heat for 5 minutes on medium until the sugar is dissolved, whisking every few minutes. Strain the shrub through a fine-mesh strainer.

CUCUMBER MARTINI

BRANCH & BARREL
4100 AVALON BOULEVARD, ALPHARETTA

Bar manager Taylor Smith adores the Minnesota-based brand Crop's Organic Cucumber Vodka for this cocktail. "It's not too sweet, not too fruity, not too sour," he says. "It just comes out perfect every time."

GLASSWARE: Coupe glass

GARNISH: Cucumber slice

- 2 oz. Crop Organic Cucumber Vodka
- 1 oz. cucumber juice
- 1 oz. fresh lime juice
- ½ oz. simple syrup

1. Combine all of the ingredients in a cocktail shaker and shake with ice.

2. Strain the cocktail into a coupe with fresh ice and garnish with a cucumber slice.

GOLDEN HOUR

FOUNDATION SOCIAL EATERY
55 ROSWELL STREET SUITE 100, ALPHARETTA

Foundation Social Eatery is a big fan of Barr Hill Gin, which is made in Vermont and incorporates raw honey. It plays nicely with the floral notes of the apricot preserves. Preserves are better to use than jam/jelly since it will have lower sugar content and, generally, more actual fruit. In the fall, Foundation uses Barr Hill Tom Cat Gin to add more complexity.

GLASSWARE: Coupe glass

GARNISH: Sprig of thyme

- 2 to 3 slices of lemon
- Thyme leaves from 3 sprigs
- Barspoon apricot preserves
- 1 oz. Barr Hill Gin
- 1 oz. Cocchi Americano
- ¾ oz. white grapefruit juice
- ½ oz. apricot liqueur

1. Place the slices of lemon, picked thyme leaves, and apricot preserves in a shaker tin and muddle to release the lemon juice and oils from the thyme.

2. Add the remaining ingredients and ice. Shake hard for 10 to 15 seconds to incorporate all of the flavors and dilute the cocktail.

3. Double-strain the cocktail into a coupe. Garnish with a sprig of thyme on the rim of the glass. Be sure to clap/slap the thyme before placing it on the glass in order to release some more of the aromas from the herbs.

RUM DRANK

FOUNDATION SOCIAL EATERY
55 ROSWELL STREET SUITE 100, ALPHARETTA

Foundation Social Eatery is a chef-driven concept in Alpharetta with a cocktail menu that's serious business. After shuttering its original location in Roswell in 2020, Foundation Social Eatery came roaring back to great success in Alpharetta. Their spacious covered patio is the perfect place to imbibe a libation or two, and diners rave as much about their talented bartenders as they do about their delicious food and stellar hospitality. Rum and pineapple are always a delicious combination, and this cocktail gets an extra dose of it with pineapple oleo, which is a great way to draw flavors from what normally would be waste.

GLASSWARE: Wineglass

GARNISH: Dehydrated lime wheel

- 1 oz. Plantation Stiggins' Fancy Pineapple Rum
- 1 oz. Fernet Francisco Manzanilla
- 1 oz. pineapple juice
- ¾ oz. fresh lime juice
- ¾ oz. Pineapple Oleo Saccharum (see recipe)
- Mint bouquet, to aromatize

1. Add all of the ingredients, except for the mint, to a shaker tin with ice. Shake hard for 10 to 15 seconds.
2. Strain the cocktail into a wineglass filled with pebble ice.
3. Be sure to slap/clap the mint to release the aromatics, then delicately rub the glass before placing the mint bouquet in the glass as a garnish. Garnish with dehydrated lime wheel.

PINEAPPLE OLEO SACCHARUM:

Cut the top and bottom off 1 pineapple. Set the top aside in order to save the fronds for future garnishes. With the pineapple situated vertically, cut the pineapple into 6 equal pieces/slices. This will help in cutting both the skin and the core out. Once you remove the pineapple skin and core, place them into a bowl on a scale and weigh it. Add an equal weight of sugar to the pineapple skin and core. Example: if the skin and core weighs 50 grams, then you would add 50 grams sugar. Then stir and lightly muddle to ensure the sugar is evenly coated over everything. Vacuum-seal the mixture and leave it out overnight. If you don't have a vacuum machine, you can cover a bowl with plastic wrap and leave it out. The next day, strain the liquid.

THE GRANTHAM

THE SELECT

6405 BLUE STONE ROAD SUITE 200, SANDY SPRINGS

The Grantham has been a mainstay at The Select since day one. The Grantham #2 is a scotch variation that beverage director Michael Kunz says is his actual favorite, but it was never ordered and ultimately nixed from the menu since Atlanta is a town that definitely prefers bourbon. Nevertheless, Kunz finds a way to sneak a tiny bit of his favorite spirit into The Grantham—a few spritzes of peated scotch (use Compass Box Peat Monster or Laphroaig Scotch).

GLASSWARE: Rocks glass

GARNISH: Rosemary sprigs, 3 spritzes peated scotch

- 2 oz. Old Forester 100 Proof Bourbon
- 1 oz. Earl Grey/Rosemary Simple Syrup (see recipe)
- ¾ oz. fresh lemon juice
- Grantham Ice Cube (see recipe)

1. Add all of the ingredients to a cocktail shaker, shake well, and double-strain the cocktail over a Grantham Ice Cube into a rocks glass.

2. Garnish with rosemary sprigs and 3 spritzes of scotch from an atomizer.

GRANTHAM ICE CUBE: Fill a 2-inch ice cube tray with 1 small sprig of rosemary, 1 lemon peel, a small amount of Earl Grey tea, then add water to fill. Freeze overnight.

EARL GREY/ROSEMARY SIMPLE SYRUP: Steep 3 bags Earl Grey tea and a good handful of rosemary in 32 oz. hot water for 5 minutes to make the tea. Strain the tea into a pot, removing the tea and rosemary in the process, then add 32 oz. white sugar (1:1 ratio with water) and bring the mixture to a boil. After you reach boiling point, remove the syrup from heat, let it rest for 5 minutes, and strain.

CIDER CIPHER (NA)

THE SELECT
6405 BLUE STONE ROAD SUITE 200, SANDY SPRINGS

The Select has a seasonally changing, European-influenced menu, and one of the most gorgeous interiors in all of Atlanta. Partner Michael Kunz, who oversees the beverage program at The Select, took a wine class his senior year of college "because it basically seemed like a great way to meet girls," but soon discovered he had an affinity for it. Over the years, he's expanded his passion to spirits as well after becoming a regular at Atlanta's Kimball House. He's curated an excellent, seasonally changing cocktail menu at The Select that continues to impress. In Cider Cipher, sage, apple, and star anise make for a delicious zero-proof fall drink.

GLASSWARE: Coupe glass

GARNISH: Star anise pod

- 2 oz. apple juice
- 1½ oz. Seedlip Spice 94
- ¾ oz. fresh lemon juice
- ½ oz. Sage Simple Syrup (see recipe)
- 1 star anise pod

1. Shake the liquid ingredients over ice with 1 star anise pod.

2. Double-strain the cocktail into a coupe and garnish with a fresh star anise pod.

SAGE SIMPLE SYRUP: Simmer together 10 sage leaves, 1 cup water, and 1 cup sugar for 10 minutes, strain, and let cool.

SUMMERTIME SETBACK

HUGO'S OYSTER BAR
10360 ALPHARETTA STREET, ROSWELL

Hugo's Oyster Bar twists the traditional Lemon Drop with fresh muddled blueberries and mint. All of their juices and mixes are freshly made in-house. Poured into a martini glass, it is a super refreshing sipper to remind you of summertime year-round.

GLASSWARE: Martini glass
GARNISH: Fresh blueberries

- **Fresh blueberries, as needed**
- **Mint, to taste**
- **2 oz. FRÏS Vodka**
- **¾ oz. fresh lemon juice**
- **¾ oz. simple syrup**

1. Muddle fresh blueberries and mint in a shaker tin with vodka, lemon juice, and syrup.

2. Strain and pour the cocktail into a martini glass. Garnish with additional fresh blueberries.

TEQUILA OLD FASHIONED

HUGO'S OYSTER BAR
10360 ALPHARETTA STREET, ROSWELL

At Hugo's, they use a unique tequila infusion in an otherwise traditional Old Fashioned.

GLASSWARE: Rocks glass

GARNISH: Dehydrated orange slice

- 2 oz. Pineapple & Vanilla–Infused Tequila (see recipe)
- ½ oz. demerara simple syrup
- 2 dashes 18.21 Grapefruit Lavender Bitters

1. Stir the tequila and syrup together in a mixing glass.

2. Pour the cocktail into a rocks glass over one large square cube.

3. Add the bitters and garnish with a dehydrated orange slice.

PINEAPPLE & VANILLA–INFUSED TEQUILA: Combine 1 pineapple, peeled, cut, and cored, with 3½ cups tequila and 1 vanilla bean, cut in half, in an airtight jar for 1 week. Strain out the fruit.

SPANISH PIPEDREAM

Falling Rabbit is a chic restaurant that takes a casual approach to fine dining. Owner Babs Woods cut her teeth in the Chicago bar scene before bringing her bartending talents to Duluth. She's constantly tinkering and creating drinks that challenge her guests' palates while also remaining approachable. New York Sours are one of Bab Woods's favorite cocktails. She started with the white port, which she had never had before, and decided to add in the oleo. It was a lot of playing around before she found the right balance, and the float is a beautiful touch.

GLASSWARE: Pilsner glass

- 1 oz. Eagle Rare 10 Year
- ¾ oz. white port
- ¼ oz. Enrico Toro Torella 72
- ¾ oz. Saffron Oleo (see recipe)
- ¾ oz. fresh lemon juice
- 2 dashes Regans' Orange Bitters No. 6
- Cabernet sauvignon, for the float

1. Shake all of the ingredients together with ice in a cocktail shaker.

2. Double-strain the cocktail into a pilsner glass over ice. Top with a cabernet sauvignon float.

SAFFRON OLEO: Combine 8 cups white sugar, 2 lemons (peeled zest only), 2 oranges (peeled zest only), 1 gram saffron, and 8 cups water. Let the saffron and citrus peels macerate in sugar overnight. Add boiling water and let the oleo cool before straining.

PLOT TWIST

When Falling Rabbit first opened, Babs Woods's guests were always asking for Martinis with olives stuffed with blue cheese, which she personally hates, as she feels they overpower the drink. The Plot Twist is her way of compromising. An olive oil fat–washed vodka forms the base, sherry replaces vermouth, and a garnish of feta-stuffed olives makes for a softer and more balanced Dirty Martini.

GLASSWARE: Coupe glass

GARNISH: 2 feta-stuffed olives, lemon twist

- 2 oz. Olive Oil–Washed Vodka (see recipe)
- ¾ oz. Herb-Infused Olive Brine (see recipe)
- ½ oz. Lustau Papirusa Manzanilla Sherry
- 2 dashes cardamom bitters
- 2 dashes Saline Solution (see recipe on page 195)

1. Chill a coupe glass. Stir all of the ingredients in a mixing glass and strain the cocktail into the chilled coupe.

2. Garnish with 2 feta-stuffed olives and a lemon twist.

OLIVE OIL–WASHED VODKA: Combine 3 tablespoons olive oil with 1 liter Castle & Key Sacred Springs Vodka. Store at room temperature for 24 hours, then freeze. Strain the solids out and bottle the vodka.

HERB-INFUSED OLIVE BRINE: Combine 6 oz. olives with brine with 2 large bunches of thyme, 2 large bunches of rosemary, 4 slightly crushed garlic cloves, 20 black peppercorns, ¼ cup honey, and 6 lemon zests. Let the mixture sit for 48 hours, then strain and save the brine.

BULLS EYE

Babs Woods adores the creamy, almost vanilla flavor of the vodka that comes from the single blade of bison grass that sits inside each vodka bottle. The Bulls Eye drinks like a Martini, but then there's a perceived sweetness from the marshmallow.

GLASSWARE: Coupe glass

GARNISH: Toasted marshmallow

- 1½ oz. Żubrówka Bison Grass Vodka
- ¾ oz. Burnt-Orange Shrub (see recipe)
- ½ oz. Brovo Witty Dry Vermouth
- ¼ oz. Amaro Nonino
- 2 dashes Regans' Orange Bitters No. 6
- 2 dashes Saline Solution (see recipe on page 195)
- Orange peel, to express

1. Chill a coupe glass. Add all of the ingredients, except for the orange peel, to a mixing glass with ice and stir.

2. Strain the cocktail into the chilled coupe, over a big rock. Express the orange peel over the drink and discard it.

3. Garnish with a toasted marshmallow.

BURNT-ORANGE SHRUB: Combine 4 ripe oranges, sliced in rings and charred on the grill, with 2 cups champagne vinegar and 2 cups white sugar. Muddle the oranges and mix until all of the sugar is dissolved. Let the shrub sit for 48 hours and strain.

BITTERSWEET SYMPHONY

FALLING RABBIT
3580 WEST LAWRENCEVILLE STREET, DULUTH

Babs Woods wanted to create a Tequila Sour for the menu, so she spent some time playing around with different shrubs and vinegars. Shoyu gives it some Asian flavor, which she balances with marigold and thyme. The end result is a little herbaceous, very light, and extremely refreshing.

GLASSWARE: Coupe glass

GARNISH: Black lime, grated

- 2 oz. thyme-infused tequila
- ½ oz. Sweet & Sour Shrub (see recipe)
- ½ oz. Marigold Syrup (see recipe)
- ¼ oz. St-Germain Elderflower Liqueur
- 2 dashes cardamom bitters
- 1 egg white

1. Chill a coupe glass. Combine all of the ingredients in a cocktail shaker without ice and dry-shake, to froth.

2. Add ice and wet-shake.

3. Double-strain the cocktail into the chilled coupe. Garnish with grated black lime.

SWEET & SOUR SHRUB: Combine 3 cups lime juice, 2 cups lemon juice, 2 cups Banyuls vinegar, and 2 cups shoyu and let the mixture sit for 24 hours.

MARIGOLD SYRUP: Combine 6 oz. calendula tea flowers, 4 cups white sugar, and 2 orange peels, stir, and let the mixture sit for 30 minutes. Add 4 cups water, bring the mixture to a boil, and let it simmer for 5 minutes. Let the syrup cool, then strain it.

IT'S STRAWBERRY THYME

UP ON THE ROOF

33 SOUTH MAIN STREET, ALPHARETTA

Atlanta loves a rooftop bar, and now, Alpharetta gets it very own with UP on the Roof. "Our experience is the view," says Wilson Oswald. "We want people to come up to UP on the Roof to be impressed by the city." With that elevated view, there needs to be an elevated drinking experience as well that can still handle volume. So how do you get drinks out quickly to folks? With batched and bottled cocktails, which has quickly become their signature. UP on the Roof bottles ingredients fresh in oxygen-reducing casks, so that patrons can get a great drink in seconds. That's a cocktail, but quick! This sweet-and-sour strawberry gin drink gets a bit of herbal loveliness from a house-made thyme syrup.

GLASSWARE: Rocks glass, single serve swing-top bottle

GARNISH: Strawberry

- 1½ oz. Fords London Dry Gin
- 1½ oz. seedless strawberry puree
- 1 oz. lemon sour
- ½ oz. Cointreau
- Barspoon Thyme Syrup (see recipe)

1. In a mixing glass, combine all of the ingredients and stir until fully mixed. Refrigerate the cocktail immediately and store until ready to drink. It can be served over ice or neat.

2. Serve in a single serve swing-top bottle. Use a whole strawberry for garnish.

THYME SYRUP: Steep 1 sprig of thyme in 2 oz. hot water for 1 hour. Strain the infusion into 2 oz. sugar and blend until the sugar is dissolved. Allow the syrup to cool.

SWEATER WEATHER

UP ON THE ROOF
33 SOUTH MAIN STREET, ALPHARETTA

Sweater Weather is a newer addition to UP on the Roof's fall and winter menu, with great complexity to it thanks to the sherry and orgeat. Just a dash of Tajín adds incredible flavor. "It's almost a seven-step cocktail," says Wilson Oswald, "but we can get it out to people fast."

GLASSWARE: Rocks glass, single serve swing-top bottle
GARNISH: 2 blackberries on a prism pick

- 1½ oz. Four Roses Bourbon
- 1¼ oz. cranberry juice
- ½ oz. Sandeman Sherry Armada Superior Cream
- ¼ oz. orgeat
- ¼ oz. blackberry simple syrup
- ¼ oz. fresh lime juice
- ½ dash Tajín

1. In a mixing glass, combine all of the ingredients and stir until fully mixed. Refrigerate the cocktail immediately and store until ready to drink. It can be served over ice or neat.

2. Serve the cocktail in a single serve swing-top bottle. Garnish with 2 blackberries on a prism pick.

TO "QUILA" MOCKINGBIRD

UP ON THE ROOF
33 SOUTH MAIN STREET, ALPHARETTA

A jalapeño and ginger simple syrup adds a sweet yet spicy element to this cocktail, and a touch of crème de violette ups the presentation.

GLASSWARE: Rocks glass

GARNISH: Jalapeño wheel

- Kosher salt, for the rim
- 1¾ oz. Casamigos Blanco Tequila
- ¾ oz. fresh lime juice
- ¾ oz. Jalapeño Ginger Simple Syrup (see recipe)
- ¼ oz. crème de violette

1. Wet the rim of a rocks glass, then dip it in kosher salt to give it a rim.

2. Combine the tequila, lime juice, and syrup in a shaking tin with ice and shake vigorously.

3. Strain the cocktail over fresh ice into the salt-rimmed rocks glass.

4. Using a barspoon, slowly add the crème de violette to the inner rim of the glass so that it sinks to the bottom, creating a beautiful layered drink.

5. Garnish with a jalapeño wheel.

JALAPEÑO GINGER SIMPLE SYRUP: Combine ¼ cup hot water, ¼ cup white sugar, ¼ cup fresh ginger, and ¼ cup jalapeños, chopped, with their seeds, in a blender and blend on high for 2 minutes. It should have a thick consistency. Use a large food-grade chinois strainer to remove pulp and seeds. Press excess liquid from the pulp.

RUSH HOUR

C&S SEAFOOD & OYSTER BAR
3930 PEACHTREE ROAD NORTHEAST, BROOKHAVEN

Rush hour in Atlanta blows, but this cocktail from C&S is better. It's both boozy and refreshing, it's full-bodied, and it makes you feel like your toes are in the sand, with a smoky finish. You can enjoy this drink at any C&S location—Sandy Springs, Brookhaven, or Vinings.

GLASSWARE: Martini glass

GARNISH: Twisted lime wheel

- Black volcanic salt, for the rim
- 1½ oz. Tres Agaves Reposado Tequila
- ¾ oz. Giffard Crème de Pamplemousse Rose
- ½ oz. fresh lime juice
- ½ oz. Mezcal District Fandango
- ¼ oz. agave nectar

1. Wet the rim of a martini glass with lime juice and dip the rim into black volcanic salt.

2. Combine all of the ingredients in a cocktail shaker with ice and shake.

3. Strain the cocktail into the martini glass. Garnish with a twisted lime wheel.

FILTHY OLD FASHIONED

C&S SEAFOOD & OYSTER BAR
3930 PEACHTREE ROAD NORTHEAST, BROOKHAVEN

You may have some maraschino cherries or Luxardo cherries hanging around in your bar cart, but C&S swears by the Filthy Black Cherrry for their Old Fashioned. Using a bit of the syrup from the jar adds the right amount of sweet and tartness, and salting the cherries as a garnish offers a little surprise.

GLASSWARE: Rocks glass

GARNISH: Flamed orange peel; Filthy Cherries, salted

- 2 oz. Michter's US 1 Kentucky Straight Bourbon
- ½ oz. Filthy Black Cherry Syrup
- 1 demerara sugar cube
- 3 dashes 18.21 Bitters Prohibition Aromatic Bitters
- 3 dashes orange bitters

1. Combine all of the ingredients in a mixing glass and stir.
2. Pour the cocktail into a rocks glass then garnish with a flamed orange peel and salted Filthy Cherries.

BEST HANGOVER MEALS IN ATLANTA

Did you overindulge in one too many Espresso Martinis last night? We've got your back with Atlanta's finest grub for even the most epic of hangovers. Put on your sunglasses and slink on into any of these fine Atlanta eateries.

HOME GROWN'S COMFY CHICKEN BISCUIT
968 MEMORIAL DRIVE SOUTHEAST

There's no headache too great that an order of Home Grown's bottomless coffee and a Comfy Chicken Biscuit can't cure. It's a big serving of fried chicken smothered in pork gravy that can easily feed two, and it'll only set you back about fourteen bucks.

TASSILI'S RAW REALITY CAFÉ'S PUNANY WRAPS
1059 RALPH DAVID ABERNATHY BOULEVARD

For the health nuts who eschew the healing powers of grease and instead like to reach for something green and healthy after a night of drinking, we recommend Tassili's Raw Reality Café on the Westside. Tassili Maat has assembled an array of delectable, good-for-you wraps stuffed with couscous, avocado, spicy mixed kale salad, and so much more deliciousness. Order ahead online to avoid a wait.

SLUTTY VEGAN'S FUSSY HUSSY BURGER
MULTIPLE LOCATIONS

A Clark Atlanta University graduate, Pinky Cole has created a total empire with her suggestively named vegan burger chain, Slutty Vegan. She originally created Slutty Vegan out of a desire to enjoy late-night vegan junk food in Atlanta, and her burgers smothered in "slut sauce" and a side of her crinkle fries seasoned with "slut dust" are just the ticket for even the most monstrous of hangovers.

Slutty Vegan

LEE'S BAKERY BANH MI AND VIETNAMESE ICED COFFEE
4005 BUFORD HIGHWAY NORTHEAST SUITE C

When it comes to food in Atlanta, you don't want to overlook Buford Highway, a corridor of global cuisines. Lee's Bakery has been much beloved in Atlanta for decades, so much so that they have sold one million of their sandwiches since 2006! You can still get their banh mi for less than ten bucks today, and their sweet Vietnamese iced coffee will wake you up, too.

WAFFLE HOUSE'S ALL STAR SPECIAL
MULTIPLE LOCATIONS

When it comes to hangovers, Atlanta folks know that the true king in this town is Waffle House. My go-to order is a medium plate of hash browns, smothered and covered, with a chocolate chip waffle and egg and cheese biscuit. But you can't go wrong with the All Star Special, which gets you a little bit of everything.

Acknowledgments

I would like to express my deepest gratitude to all of the incredibly talented bartenders and restaurant owners who participated in this book. It's your immense talent, skills, and passion that make this city one of the best places in the world to live—and to drink!

Special thanks to the team at Cider Mill Press for their patience and support throughout this process. After years of writing articles online, it feels surreal to be able to put something on my bookshelf that has my name on it.

I am indebted to my parents who have supported me through everything in life and always encouraged me to write. To you both, I owe everything.

To my partner Davis and my shih tzu, Gravy, thank you for staying by my side through many late nights. You both are the loves of my life.

Finally, thank you to Atlanta for being the best place in the world to call my home. This is my love letter to you.

About the Author

Trisha Pintavorn is a marketing professional and "high-calorie content creator" for Atlanta Eats, a local media company covering Atlanta's food and drink scene. She has a Bachelor of Science from Georgia Tech and an MBA from Emory University. When she's not sipping and savoring her way through Atlanta, you can find her at home watching delightfully trashy reality TV with her partner, Davis, and their shih tzu, Gravy.

Photo Credits

Pages 16–17, 297 by Andrew Thomas Lee; page 25 by Caleb Jones; pages 30–31, 36, 124–125 by Brandon Amato; pages 33, 34, 126, 129 by Sarah Newman; page 49 Chris Avedissian; page 73 by Graham Johnson; pages 81, 85, 349, 350, 366 by Sharon Benton for Atlanta Eats' Order Up Social; page 99 by Becca Mamane for Atlanta Eats' Order Up Social; page 136 courtesy of Atelier Media; page 190 by Cameron Greene; pages 202, 284, 287, 288 by Mobs Robertson; page 247 by Mia Yakei; page 294 by Jose Pereiro; page 297 by Andrew Thomas Lee; page 298 by Tyler Bonn; page 341 by Lauren Lizz Photography.

Pages 9, 10 courtesy of Library of Congress.

Pages 1, 3, 4–5, 6, 14, 20–21, 92–93, 150–151, 238–239, 300–301 used under official license from Shutterstock.com.

All other images courtesy of the respective bars, restaurants, and interviewees.

MEASUREMENT CONVERSIONS

	1 dash		0.625 ml
	4 dashes		2.5 ml
	1 teaspoon		5 ml
¼ oz.			7.5 ml
⅓ oz.	2 teaspoons		10 ml
½ oz.	3 teaspoons	1 tablespoon	15 ml
⅔ oz.	4 teaspoons		20 ml
¾ oz.			22.5 ml
17⁄20 oz.			25 ml
1 oz.		2 tablespoons	30 ml
1 ½ oz.		3 tablespoons	45 ml
1 ¾ oz.			52.5 ml
2 oz.	4 tablespoons	¼ cup	60 ml
8 oz.		1 cup	250 ml
16 oz.	1 pint	2 cups	500 ml
24 oz.		3 cups	750 ml
32 oz.	1 quart	4 cups	1 liter (1,000 ml)

Index

—About Cider Mill Press Book Publishers—

Good ideas ripen with time. From seed to harvest, Cider Mill Press brings fine reading, information, and entertainment together between the covers of its creatively crafted books. Our Cider Mill bears fruit twice a year, publishing a new crop of titles each spring and fall.

"Where Good Books Are Ready for Press"
501 Nelson Place
Nashville, Tennessee 37214
cidermillpress.com